THE SCIENCE OF LEADERSHIP

THE SCIENCE of LEADERSHIP

The Manager of the Third Millennium

VICTORIA C. DEPAUL
THOMAS MICHAEL POWELL

GALILEO BUSINESS & LEARNING CONSULTANTS LLC • AUBURN, MA

THE SCIENCE OF LEADERSHIP

Published by Galileo Business & Learning Consultants LLC

ISBN   978-0-9794508-0-8

Cover Layout/Interior Design: Spring Hoteling
Interior Graphics: Leon Mitchell Powell
Back Cover Photo: Louis Burwick

Attention: Corporations and Schools. This book is available at quantity discounts with bulk purchase for educational, business or sales promotional use. For information, please write to: Galileo Business & Learning Consultants LLC, 482 Southbridge St, Suite 205, Auburn, Massachusetts, 01501. Please supply quantity, how the book will be used, and the date needed. Requests can also be sent to info@GalileoConsultants.com

Table of Contents

INTRODUCTION

_The typical office in the
United States is a dangerous place._

In this age of road-rage, and now desk-rage, if you are employed, your safety is at risk. As stress levels are escalated, employees are increasingly fueled by anger, resentment, pessimism, frustration, anxiety, distrust and other negative emotions. As a manager employed by a major telecommunications company I am no stranger to workplace violence. Some years ago a disgruntled employee, with a history of instability called the office to report his intention to kill a manager. While law officials and company security worked to apprehend the employee, all managers on site were confined to a darkened conference room with shades drawn for our own safety. In this case, police were able to locate the employee before he took action. He explained that he was angry and didn't know how to vent his frustration. That same year our office was subject to bomb threats, employee breakdowns, out of control absenteeism, extensive turn-over rates, and an overall climate of chaos.

The term 'desk-rage' coined some years ago, refers to a growing phenomenon of unstable, unpredictable and explosive behaviors occurring in the workplace. While cases of extreme workplace hostility and violence are likely to receive widespread news coverage, less extreme, yet just as severe, incidents of aggression, rebellion and conflict are commonplace. If you hold a leadership or supervisory position your challenges are twofold: attempting to meet increasing production and service demands while coping with a workforce increasingly incapable to support these demands.

Most people, at all ranks and levels of an organization, spend more than half of their waking life at work. The anxiety that employees experience in the workplace added to the stresses that they encounter away from the job result in a severely diminished workforce. The result is that organizations experience a major loss of productivity, ineffective communications and increased job dissatisfaction. All of this translates to increased expenditures in the form of tardiness, absenteeism, high turn-over rates, high employee training costs and equipment neglect and failures. Further, overall poor performance continues to reduce profit margins even more. Take a look at the following list to see if your organization has any of these symptoms:

- Emotional reactivity between employees
- Flare ups of anger, hostility, exchanges of insults
- Interpersonal aversions, resistances, and conflicts
- Arguments, quarreling, disputes that result in

strained relationships
- Jealousies, power and turf struggles, infighting, backbiting
- Ego: A person acting like they are better than others, using overt or subtle put downs of others
- Dictator mentality: someone preaching to others how they should BE
- Victim mentality: "Everybody is picking on me, everybody is against me —especially management"
- Poor leadership, due either to ignorance or to personality problems (like ego or dictator)
- Reduced, slowed, withheld, and lost communications
- Low morale and motivation, indifference, lethargy
- Negative attitudes towards management or the organization
- Reduced responsibility and initiative: "I am not responsible for anything; I just work here"
- Reduced creativity and initiative
- Indifference to the mission and goals of the organization
- Poor compliance with Safety and Corporate policies
- Mis-ordered priorities
- Tardiness and absenteeism
- Gossip and rumors
- Insecurity, lack of trust and confidence, fear
- Feelings of powerlessness, hopelessness
- Lack of cooperation and support between people and departments
- Resentments, retaliations and revenge
- Resistance, rebellion, sabotage

- Mistakes, omissions, errors, all leading to break-downs
- Poor job satisfaction
- Low personnel retention, high general turnover
- Loss of your best people due to the Negative Energy climate of the workplace
- Loss of customers due to poor customer service
- In short, chaos in your organization resulting in poor departmental and poor overall performance, production, and therefore increased expenditures leading to reduced profits

The above symptoms are classic in the workplace. Think of the above list as "Symptoms of a Dysfunctional Organization". If your organization is experiencing any of the symptoms above your organization is not performing at peak levels. The above symptoms are classic in the American workplace.

For almost 24 years I was employed in the telecommunications industry, what was known as the Bell System. Anyone who is familiar with the former Bell System knows that this is the end result of several regional and nation-wide company mergers. I began my career with a regional Bell Company as a service representative in customer service. Through hard work, and some now might say hard luck, I was promoted within three years of hire.

Ah, those were the good ole days. Or were they? Exactly how efficient was the organization? Recall our list of "Symptoms of a Dysfunctional Organization." Every item on that list comes from personal experience and observation from my management years. As supervisors and managers in the 80's it was our primary duty to remind employees that "You don't have to work here. You get to work here." We lived and worked in a climate of "Shape Up or Ship Out".

Everything was black and white with absolutely no gray areas. Those who called out sick with terminal cancer were disciplined according to the same process as those out sick with a cold. Interesting for a company that boasted unlimited paid sick days. Yes, if you were ill you could call in for a sick day but the consequences for doing so were severe, often leading to harassment and micromanagement. I always found it curious, however, that even with such stringent controls, absenteeism and tardiness have been and continue to be an issue for management. Even more curious, these acts were usually performed by repeat offenders.

For the most part, managers were taught, by example, to be workplace bullies, myself included. As workplace bullies we managed by intimidation, threats, public humiliation and at times outright hostility. Of course this behavior wasn't taught in management or leadership training nor was it overtly encouraged. So if these behaviors were not condoned, why then did they persist? Why does this management tactic still flourish in our businesses and corporations today?

In response, I suggest the following:

1) Managers do not know another style.

2) Business leaders are interested in the short-term end result, not the path to get there.

3) Managers and supervisors receive passive rewards for

their aggressive behavior with bonuses, increased salaries, compensation time and other benefits.

4) Leaders, managers and supervisors do not understand what really motivates people to operate at peak potential.

Let's consider each of these points.

1) Managers do not know another style.

If you are a manager or supervisor consider your own management style. Where does it come from? For those of us promoted from the ranks as I was, often we mirror the behaviors and actions of our own managers and supervisors. Chances are if you were promoted based on positive results in your non-management position little or no attention was paid to whether you had the skills necessary to be an effective manager or leader. The Peter Principle could be at work here: you were very good at what you did and so were promoted into a higher position and level of responsibility. However, newly promoted managers often do not have or receive adequate training for the entirely different responsibilities of the new position, and so are, in effect, promoted into a condition of incompetence.

If you were hired through a college recruitment process certainly you come to the organization with the benefits of your formal education but that did not necessarily include training, much less experience in negotiation and interpersonal skills. Educational degrees or technical expertise in a particular function does not ensure that an employee can effectively lead a workgroup—an interpersonal skill.

While management skills can be developed, in this day and age of reduced training budgets, limited training dollars are often reserved for those newly hired into non-management functions. This trend leaves leaders and managers without the training support necessary to be effective in their positions as motivators and supporters of others.

In the 80's at the time I was newly promoted to management, the company had an established training curriculum for new managers and a continuation curriculum for current managers. In the 90's, in an effort to save money, courses were either eliminated or trimmed down to the level where they were essentially useless. As we advanced into the third millennium, many training courses were shifted to a multimedia format; which while better than nothing, did not approach the quality of training offered 20 years ago.

Regardless of the quality of any management training curriculum, the climate of your workplace is established by its leaders. Furthermore, a company can provide the best training that money can buy, but unless it supports its implementation outside of the classroom it will have little effect on the vital area of leadership and management.

So, in the absence of a formal training program of substance, managers and supervisors fall back on the examples and tutelage available to them—and hence the problem as they seek guidance from teammates equally unskilled in the synergy of effective organizations, how to manage people and how to manage their own negative behaviors.

2) *Business leaders are interested in the short-term end result, not the path to get there.*

Let's face it. In these tough, economic times the dollar rules. Businesses are constantly faced with how to produce more with less. "More" translates to increased profits while "Less" means reduced expenses. In order to decrease expenses each year budgets are cut leaving companies and departments to operate with reduced resources. To satisfy company leaders, stakeholders and customers, businesses will sacrifice long-term success strategies in favor of short-term, immediate pay-offs. Since labor is one of the major expenses of any organizational budget, increasingly more businesses are choosing to trim costs through downsizing, mergers, collaborations and out-sourcing–all of these ultimately establishing a reduction in human capital.[1] While these strategies may boost the bottom line in the short-term, profits to the company and dividends to stockholders, are leaders considering the total cost to the long-term survival of the organization?

Here I must make one point that is absolutely essential to the understanding of the remainder of this work. Human capital is the most critical resource to any organization. Unfortunately, for most organizations it is the most disposable. Consider this: People are the ultimate source of energy and therefore the Power of an organization.

It is people who perform all of the thinking, planning and designing. It is people that operate your machinery, interact with each other and interface with customers. Reductions in human capital, designed to alleviate a present financial condition, will

---

1 This does not refer to strategic consolidation efforts designed to streamline processes and job functions which will increase the overall efficiency of the organization. Such strategies are a necessary component of effective leadership. In my experience, however, budget cuts are the major criteria motivating present action, with little regard to the effect on day to day operations or long-term objectives.

result in a reduction in the Power of your organization. This reduction in Power, in the long-term, will affect the organization's ability to maintain and achieve current goals, retain and attract customers and compete effectively in your marketplace.

3) *Managers and supervisors receive passive rewards for their aggressive behavior with bonuses, increased salaries, compensation time and other benefits.*

In many cases management compensation is dependent upon the bottom line success of the organization. As a manager, this means that salary is directly related to the performance of those reporting to me. While the positive intent of this pay structure is to increase management accountability throughout the organization, those without strong, positive interpersonal and management skills will resort to coercive techniques in order to meet team and company objectives.

Managers are not held accountable for how they achieve their results, just whether or not the goal is met. Throughout my early career I have seen managers and supervisors, myself included, rewarded for their harassment of employees. Unfortunately, in my current work with organizations, I observe that this behavior is still routine today. There is a wide separation of bonuses and benefits between management and the ranks. With so much at stake, often managers will do whatever necessary to meet the mark.

4) *Leaders, managers and supervisors do not understand what really motivates people to operate at peak potential.*

In order to achieve results, managers lead by harassment,

threats, and manipulation through both covert and overt means. While not openly sanctioned, this management style remains common as company leaders remain focused on bottom line results and employees remain silent. Employees will endure on-the-job intimidation for a variety of reasons including:

- Fear of repercussions including termination
- Fear of termination leading to loss of income, healthcare, pension and other benefits
- Belief that Leadership doesn't care anyway
- Belief that it probably isn't going to be any better elsewhere

Businesses continue to struggle to achieve adequate results because managers and supervisors do not understand how organizational energy systems operate. Add to this the fact that managers do not understand the fundamental principles that fuel human motivation and the end result is the list stated above.

In the pages that follow you will be introduced to a powerful technology of personal and organizational change. You will learn that businesses are Energy Systems and operate much like Energy Systems that you are already familiar with.

I learned of this leadership and personal achievement model four years ago. By this time I had survived several company mergers. The work culture of my last corporate position made the informal implementation of this model painless, at least within the human resources division. This company places an emphasis on effective communication, the value of the individual, and teamwork. As a nationwide company with over 210,000 employees I can't state with absolute certainty that all departments and divisions shared the same level of commitment to creating a work climate that is team-based. I do know that as a human resources manager I met with no resistance; the HR leadership team echoed this message so the gate was wide open for change.

While the objectives were clear, how to accomplish this wasn't always so apparent. Promoted into a new leadership position, I inherited a team that demonstrated most of the symptoms of a dysfunctional organization that are listed on page 2. As I began to identify and list the problems with this team, it became clear exactly what the problem was. This team was attempting to produce positive results while operating in Negative Energies, a strategy sure to fail.

The primary issue was the Dictator mentality of all but one of the managers. Employees were made to believe that they were indeed 'subordinate' a term that for many suggests 'less than', inferior or secondary. Because of this possible connotation I do not use the word, preferring employee, partner, associate or team member— which is more accurate anyway, at least if your organization desires to operate at peak potential. Employees were micro-managed, bordering on harassment. The work environment showed a clear division of 'us' versus 'them' with frequent meetings behind closed doors. The overall result was a de-motivated team operating in distrust and discontent. In this environment the primary focus of these employees was to not get fired. In addition to the low morale I discovered that the Dictator mentality extended far beyond the office. The client base was dissatisfied, offering numerous complaints, regularly dismissed by the management team. The prevailing thought was "we are unique and you need us, we don't need you." Of course this was and is a costly mistake; in business you are rarely the only game in town.

In short order I began the task of turning things around. I recognized the significance of each individual to accomplishing the end result. Over the years I have learned that people want to work. People want to contribute. Understanding this and giving them the opportunity to do so is all that is needed to move any team to success.

Upon completing this book, you will have learned how to implement strategies and processes that will be a powerful agent of Positive Energy for your organization. But of far more significance to you, your family, and the global community you will discover that the true power in life comes from understanding how life works and how you (and others) can create life as you would desire. If you want new and different results, you need new and different ideas. You must release the human potential that lies dormant in your organization and that lies dormant within you.

CHAPTER 1

_____

Human Quantum Energy

To begin, an understanding of the following terms is necessary:

Energy:

Everything that exists is energy. There isn't anything else but energy. Life is about energy. It runs on energy; it seeks energy; it transforms energy. This includes apparently solid matter in the physical universe. Even 'solid' matter is but energy maintaining a fixed pattern instead of flowing or radiating. Note that there are two very distinct kinds of energies in our lives. Physical energies are all those that are produced by physical means.

Physical forms of energy are many including: mechanical, electrical, potential, kinetic, gravitational, chemical, thermodynamic, nuclear, light, rotational, electromagnetic radiation (includes light, heat, infra red, radio, microwaves), biological, meteorological (lightning, storms, ocean heat), to name a few. Money itself is but a store and representation of energy. Notice that all of the above forms of energy are physical. All of the above forms of energy are generated by physical means, and can be measured with physical, scientific instruments.

There are also many kinds of non-physical or Quantum Energy. An energy is classified as a Quantum Life Energy when it cannot be produced by physical means or measured by scientific instruments. Such energies are Life Energies; they are produced, perceived, and used by people, Life entities. You can't go down to the local hardware store and say, "Give me a pound of love, a quart of intelligence, and a bag of happiness"

The forms of Human Quantum Energy, of Life Energy, include will, consciousness, mental energy, emotional energy, human communications and relationships. The sounds or the words on paper that we make to communicate are physical energies; but what we communicate: information, ideas, feelings, beliefs, values, desires, needs, are non-physical, Quantum Energies. Likewise, information, knowledge, intelligence, creativity, intuition are also Quantum Energies. Information may be represented physically with letters on this page, or 1 and 0's in a computer memory, but the information itself is mental energy.

You operate on energy. At the end of a day you are usually tired, of low-energy, and must sleep to recharge your life energy. You awaken in the morning full of energy for a new day, or charged with Negative Energy if you are unhappy with your life situation. You may think that is a purely physical, biological energy recharge, but it is much more than that. It is also a recharge of consciousness and will, of the Quantum Life Energy of which you are made. Your mind operates with energy. Every thought, every idea, datum, memory, image, vision, or plan is an energy form, molded by the energy of your will, and perceived by the energy that is your consciousness.

Your emotions are energies. Joy, passion, love, enthusiasm, satisfaction, monotony, indifference, anger, fear, anxiety, rage, worry, guilt, resentment, hate, sorrow, loneliness, sadness, grief, desperation, depression – all of these are energies. Pain and suffering; love and happiness are all energies.

Critical to your power in life is to understand that the most important energies of all are the Human Quantum Energies within the individual: mind, feelings and your interactions with others. These are the Energies that most affect and control the individual, the family, groups, and organizations. As we shall see, they are the most powerful energies that exist. Power is the ability to produce the desired results in any area of life, and for any person or any group. As Quantum Energy is the most powerful of all Energies, your Power in life depends on your ability to control your Quantum Energies.

The ultimate motivation of life is more and more Positive Energy, and less and less Negative Energy. This is the ultimate motivation of your organization, of every employee and of every stakeholder. To produce these experiences in your life, you must learn how these forms of energy work. You, as a person– are not your body, but your spirit. As spirit, you are a non-physical, animated, Life entity. You are a Life-Energy entity of Consciousness, Awareness and Will. You the BEing operate with non-physical, Quantum Energies of many kinds: mental, emotional, communicational, visionary, motivational, intuitional, and sentimental and more. As all that exists is energy, all force, work, change and movement are energy at work.

Polarity:

Most forms of energy are a Polarity Spectrum with both a positive and a negative side. Positive Energy is that which contributes to Power by producing, supporting and contributing to the desired results. Negative Energy is that which subtracts or reduces Power by causing frictions, blocks, damages, or destruction to an energy system.

Examples of Negative Energy within people include frustration, anger, fear, hostility, anxiety, rage, worry, guilt, sorrow, loneliness, sadness, grief, desperation, impatience, depression, etc. Examples of Negative Energy from and between individuals in groups include: personal frictions, dislikes, resentments, hate, anger attacks, blame, invalidation, jealousy, gossip, rumors, reduced or no communication, reduced or no cooperation. Examples of Negative Energy in organizations include indifference, low morale and motivation, tardiness and absenteeism, lack of caring and negligence, dishonesty, theft, suppressive leadership, retaliations, and sabotage. Negative Energy in organizations also results in high turnover and continuous employee training, all resulting in increased cost to the business.

All forms of Negative Energy in an energy system work to reduce the power, the total output of the energy system (organization) in both quantity and quality. To improve the productivity of an energy system, you must first eliminate the Negative Energy. It is impossible to sustain an increase of Positive Energy, and therefore power, in an energy system without first removing the Negative Energy. The Negative Energy causes leakage and losses of the Positive Energy, like trying to fill up a water bucket full of holes.

The basic unit, the basic "chip" (to use an electronic or computer analogy) of all energy systems is the individual human being. The individual person is the generator of all non-physical, Negative Energy in an energy system. To stop the Negative Energy in any energy system whether it be the world, nations, communities, businesses, groups, families or individuals, you must eliminate the generation of the Negative Energy within the basic "chip". The only way to eliminate Negative Energy from groups and organizations is to stop the generation of Negative Energy in and from each person.

The origin of all non-physical negative energy is a specific malfunction or "virus" in the Human Operating System: the set of subconscious programs[2] and beliefs that people have absorbed growing up. These erroneous ideas about how life works interfere with a person's ability to achieve significant levels of Positive Energy and therefore personal Power.

Life Energy is the nucleus of the human spirit itself, thus the term: Human Nuclear Energy. As you continue to read you will discover what Human Nuclear Energy is. One of its principle characteristics is that it is a polarity with positive and negative sides. When a person does not understand how it works, s/he will often generate Negative Energy instead of the Positive Energy that s/he seeks. This ignorance is the origin of all Negative

---

2 Program: A mental model, a self-created idea of how things and people should or should not be.

Energy in an organization.

Universal Law:

The Ultimate Motivation of all of Life is to achieve higher and higher levels of Positive Energy and less and less Negative Energy.

Understanding and controlling Human Nuclear Energy is the key to Positive Energy and therefore Personal Power. Armed with this knowledge you will increase your personal happiness, enjoy greater job satisfaction, create meaningful relationships and achieve significant results in your organization.

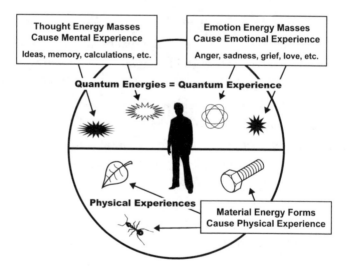

Experience is either Quantum or Physical

POWER

Power is defined as the ability to produce the desired results. Be sure to make note of this definition to avoid confusion with other ideas about power such as authority, force, political, or military power. Here Personal Power means your ability to produce whatever you want in life, and this is best achieved by using power with, not power over others.

Over the centuries, man has come out of living in caves to exercise great power over the physical universe. You live today with more power and security than even kings of 100 years ago. You command great quantities of energy.

- Your carriage has 200 horsepower instead of eight. Turn on all the lights in your typical house and you have up to 100,000 candlepower of lights.
- You communicate instantly around the world, and are able to see what is happening on the other side even as it happens.
- You fly through the air at velocities believed impossible a hundred years ago and do so in more comfort than any magic carpet. (Desert heat and sandstorms are hell on a magic carpet; lacking as they do windshields and air-conditioning.)
- Montezuma had to send runners to climb the volcanoes outside of Mexico City everyday to bring him ice because there was no way to preserve it in the heat of Mexico. You open a magical box in your kitchen, where you not only have ice 24/7, but also exquisite foods from around the world.

- Not all their riches and power could save Cleopatra or Marie Antoinette from the pains of childbirth, the ravishes of small pox or the agony of a toothache.
- You use computers for work and for play with the ability to complete complex transactions at a rate of billions of instructions per second.

So you are indeed powerful compared, not only to the average person in the past, but to kings and emperors. Where does that power come from? It comes from knowledge, from science. The climb out of the caves to the heights of mankind's power today is the history of the accumulation of knowledge.

This is also true for the power that you will acquire by reading this book. You will acquire power to handle the Quantum Energies of your life and of your family, groups and organizations. This Knowledge, and therefore Power, will allow you to recognize and stop the generation of Negative Energy in yourself and in your organization, and to enter into a continual spiral of ever increasing Positive Energy in life.

All energy is universal and acts according to universal laws. All energy, both physical and non-physical, obeys laws and principles. Life is never random; everything obeys the Laws of Cause and Effect. Physics, chemistry, and electronics obey the laws of physical energy. Emotions, thoughts and ideas, as do all Quantum Energies, obey the laws of the Quantum Universe.

Here are some examples of the Laws of Human Quantum Energy that you will learn in this book. These will be explained in further detail later in the text.

- Energy that flows, discharges and discreates.

- Resistance Causes Persistence. Resistance is any kind of Negative Energy sent against something to stop, change, punish, or destroy it.
- Energy flows to SPace[3], a point of no energy.
- Life and everything that exists and occurs in it are energy and energy processes.
- Life consists of two kinds of energy: physical and Quantum.

Knowledge is Power. In the same way that knowledge of how physical Energy works has given mankind power over the physical universe, knowledge of how the Quantum Universe works will increase power, Personal Power. Knowledge of how Quantum Energy works, will give you power over your life and allow you to be a positive flow of energy to your organization. It will give you the power to produce more of the things you want in life, both personally and in your organization.

Energy Systems:

Your business or organization is an Energy System. Understanding it from this perspective will unlock for you new levels of power and control. Energies rarely work alone. A single kind of energy working alone can produce only very limited results. Energies combine and synergize to work together in Energy Systems, which in turn are composed of sub-systems. "Synergize" means to create synergy. Synergy is the alignment, cooperation,

---

3 SPace is the absence of energy, especially Negative Energy. The first two letters are capitalized to indicate its importance as a concept. It will be discussed in a later chapter in detail.

synchronization of different energies to increase power, to produce results that would otherwise be impossible. Power is the result of the synergy of Energies.

To clarify the concept of Energy Systems, listed below are the names of some systems you are familiar with along with some of the energy subsystems that compose the greater systems. In each case, the list of energies named includes only a few of the subsystems contained in that Energy System.

Plants:

The root subsystem supports the plant and takes in water and minerals from the earth. The stem or trunk moves water and minerals up to the leaves, where photosynthesis takes place using light and chemical energy. The resulting nutrients are then distributed to all parts of the plant, including back down into the root, for growth. The root growth of some plants, rubber trees to name one, is so powerful that it can break up, or break through, 6 inches of concrete.

The Planet:

Air, water, land. The alternating polarity energy systems of light & dark and heat & cold of the sun generate energy and therefore power. There is the horizontal circulatory system of the winds, and the vertical rise and fall system caused by differing air temperatures. These differing air temperatures cause the horizontal circulatory and vertical rise and fall of the winds. Manifestations of that energy-power include all weather, thunderstorms, tornados, hurricanes, typhoons, etc. The oceans circulate and also rise and fall according to heating and cooling by the sun. The air is a subsystem of the planet and consists of many subsystems. For example, animals and humans convert oxygen to carbon dioxide; plants convert the carbon dioxide back to oxygen. The land consists of topsoil, subsoil, strata, bedrock, and magna, each with a purpose in the grand scheme of things. All of these systems working together make life possible.

Animals and the human body:

These life forms have so many energies and subsystems that just naming them all with no description whatsoever is a challenge. Some of the main ones are: skeletal system, muscular and motor systems, the blood circulatory system of which the heart is a complicated subsystem, nervous system, food intake, taste, and mastication system (i.e. mouth), digestive system, eliminatory system, perception and sensing subsystems: vision, hearing, smell, touch, taste, lymphatic system, immune system, internal temperature generation and maintenance system, respiratory system, of which the lungs are a subsystem.

Every organ is a subsystem of a greater system and in turn is itself composed of subsystems. The heart, for example, is part of the blood circulatory system, and includes a muscular system, a conduit system, a valve system, its own blood supply system and it own nervous and electrical system that controls its beat rate. The human energy system creates and operates other Energy Systems, including families, neighborhoods, cities, nations and business organizations.

On a simpler level, every tool and machine that we make is an Energy System. Even a hammer is a system: it has a handle, a shaft, and a head, each with its own purpose; and it requires a human body system to aim and operate it. It is an extension of people as energy systems permitting them to leverage energy and so do more work.

An automobile is a complex Energy System with a structural system, frame systems, rolling system, steering system, transmission system, braking system, electrical system with a lighting subsystem, climate control system. One of its subsystems is the motor, which in turn consists of many subsystems, such as starting, fuel, air, ignition, lubrication, cooling, electrical generation, electrical storage, valves, timing, among others.

A computer is a complex Energy System. It includes many subsystems: power supply system, motherboard system, storage system, input system (consisting of a mouse, keyboard, USB devices), CD and DVD drives. It also includes an output system which can consist of a visual display, printer, speakers, or network. A motherboard, in turn, has many subsystems starting with the: central processor, its cooling system, its electrical supply, video and sound chips, input and output chips, and so on. The system and its subsystem operate with many forms of electrical energies. These in turn are modulated and transformed by the chips to what ever kind of energy is needed, including digital magnetic impulse energy for the hard drive, and display control energies for the screen.

Notice again, how Power, the ability to do work and produce the desired results, comes from Energy Systems. Systems combine and align things and energies with dynamic cooperation and support; each making its particular contribution to the whole. The whole is more than the sum of the parts, but without all the parts, the whole is nothing. The same is true for your business.

People Energy Systems:

Plants, animals, the earth, tools, machinery, computers, vehicles, transport systems, electronic and communications systems are far from the only Energy Systems on the planet. Every person is a complex Energy System comprised of both physical energies and Human Quantum Energies. People then combine and synergize their energies to create extremely complex organizational energy systems: groups, corporations, non-profits, universities, and governments, to name a few. A Human Energy System exists any time two or more people get together and combine efforts towards some common goal. These Human Energy Systems are the creators of all man-made energy systems mentioned above—and of your business.

Every group of people, which includes a couple, a family, a work group or team, a small business, a huge corporation, a non-profit organization, a church, a political party, a government, a society, and a nation, is a Human Energy System. Human Energy Systems intake, transport, use, transform and output energies of many kinds and forms. Every such group is an alignment of individual energies towards common goals and purposes. Group or Organizational Energy Systems synergize and concentrate energies of all kinds, human and physical, to create enough Power to achieve things far beyond the power of lesser energy systems.

The definition of power, remember, is the ability to produce the desired results.

As one final example of an Energy System consider NASA; it includes most of the Human Energy Systems named above, including its own government, and has demonstrated the power to put a man on the moon. You do the math here: How many kinds of energy are found in the Human Energy System known as NASA, an organization that has the power to put a human being on the moon? Don't forget to include: financial energy, physical energies including light, heat, cold, electrical, and computational. Don't forget all solid matter, including materials, tools and machines. Also include all the human energies such as all thought, planning, communication, teamwork, and emotional energy. A hint with the first one–the financial energy intake for just one year: NASA's budget is about $17 billion dollars for 2007. The entire list will have many thousands of kinds of energy and matter organized in almost innumerable subsystems.

The point is that almost everything that exists is an Energy System. Some are natural, like living things, including the human being. People then group together to form Human Energy Systems, groups and organizations of all kinds. The purpose of Human Energy Systems is always Power, and they indeed have it, demonstrated by their creation of many kinds of Energy Systems such as tools, machinery, electrical systems, refrigerators, automobiles, computers, and moon rockets.

Your organization is a Human Energy System. The nature of Human Energy Systems, particularly the causes of Negative Energy and malfunctions is the subject of this book. Here is an important point: All energy obeys precise laws and principles. This includes people and all Human Energy Systems (organizations).

This means that the Energy System that is your organization, and the Energy System that is each individual in your organization, functions according to certain laws. By understanding these laws, you acquire control over the energy not only within you, but in your organization as well. You acquire the Power to eliminate Negative Energy and increase the Positive Energy.

Summary to this Point:

Everything POWERful that exists is an Energy System. An Energy System is any structure, physical or human, that combines, synergizes and concentrates energies to create the POWER to produce desired results. All groups and organizations are Human Energy Systems. You, others, your couple relationship, your family, your groups and teams, and your company are all Energy Systems. Your understanding of life as Energy Systems and your knowledge of the Laws of Human Energy will bring you Power.

The Human Quantum Energy System

Power comes from knowledge. As distinction is the father of knowledge, and therefore of Power, what follows will distinguish the existence of the internal, Human Quantum Energy System. Your non-physical, spiritual, Quantum Energies include:

- Your will and will-power, which include decision, commitment, determination, constancy, and persistence.
- Your awareness and consciousness of both self and others. Every day you consume this energy while

you are awake and recharge it in your sleep.

- Your mind and all its varieties of thought-frequency energies. These include ideas, data and knowledge, values, memories, goals, desires, mental images of the past and visions of possible futures, plans and beliefs. You also have your mental activities and abilities such as intelligence, analysis, comparison, imagination, intuition, creativity, design and planning. All of the above are Energies and Energy-powered processes.

- Your subconscious mind and all that is in it. It is thousands of times bigger than your conscious mind.

- Your emotions. Your emotions are energies and include: joy, love, enthusiasm, satisfaction, boredom, frustration, anger, fear, hostility, anxiety, rage, worry, guilt, resentment, hate, sorrow, loneliness, sadness, grief, desperation, impatience, depression, among others. Here, in the emotional energies, are found the roots of morale and motivation in families, groups and organizations.

- Your relationship with yourself defined by your self-image and your self-esteem. These define the energies that form your character and your personality. All of these are energy programs and recordings; they are part of your human "software" that programs your thinking, feeling, and doing. They determine the differences between how individuals think, feel, act, and react to the world.

- Your energies that form and affect your relationships with others. These include what you say as well as how you say it; that is, the energy you use when you communicate. Your relationships energies include your integrity, sincerity, and honesty, and how win-win you play with others. It includes how you treat others and how you respond or react to their treatment of you.

While there may be physical actions involved with these characteristics of relationships, the meanings, impulses, and motivations behind them are internal, non-physical energies. Do these energies exist? Are any of these energies going on inside of you, in your experience[4]? Are any of these energies occurring in the people around you? Do you see these in action in your spouse, your children, your family and relatives? Are any of these energies affecting the teamwork and performance of groups you participate in at work? Are any of these energies affecting, positively or negatively, the performance, power, and production of your organization? Absolutely.

All of these energies are occurring not only in you, but also in others, in all groups, and in all organizations. You experience, you perceive and feel; you live daily with all of these energies, right? We all do, and so does every group and organization composed of people. Are these energies important in life? Obviously,

---

4 Definition of "experience": Anything that you are perceiving, sensing, thinking, or feeling in the present moment particularly your experience of quantum energies. If it is necessary to refer to physical experience, what is perceived through the body, it will be stated as "physical experience". When referring to an action or event learned in the past, such as an experience in driving a car, it will be referred to as "past experience".

they are. They control us, and we control most of the other Energy Systems.

Are they complex? What happens to the complexity of the organizational energy system when you have many people involved? If you consider the quantity and complexity of your Quantum Energies (mind, thoughts, emotions, feelings, motivations, behaviors, likes and dislikes) and that every human being has more or less the same quantity and complexity; and then add into the equation all the possible interactions of all the energies of all people in your organization, the complexity exceeds that of a space shuttle. In fact, the space shuttles were created by and with Human Quantum Energies. That is its primary source of energy, not the electricity in its batteries or the fuel in its tanks.

So, yes they are complex. But– they obey rigid laws and principles, those of cause and effect. These are understandable and they are controllable. Furthermore, we can trace the root cause of all the non-physical energies (emotions, thoughts, and behaviors) down to just three fundamental energies that make up the energy nucleus of every human spirit.

Critical to your success in life is your understanding of the importance of Energy Systems, and of understanding Life and organizations in terms of energy and Energy Systems. The human being—the being or spirit part, not the body—is an Energy System. It is not physical energy: it is non-physical or Human Quantum Energy, but no less important or any less powerful— quite the contrary.

The Human Quantum Energy System, the individual person, is the most powerful energy system that exists. It is the creator of all other man-made energy systems, and it is the basic "chip" or "circuit" that comprises and operates all other man-made Energy Systems including your organization, your community, your family, for example. It is the Human Quantum Energies that create and operate all groups and organizations, which in turn create and operate all tools, instruments, and machines, from a simple hammer, to a can opener, to a nuclear reactor to a spaceship.

It is important to understand that the Human Quantum Energy System (mind, emotions and behaviors) is a coherent system. It is not just a collection of unconnected, unrelated, accidental, or randomly-occurring energies. All energies, both physical and Quantum, operate according to exact laws and principles. Everything that happens and exists in the Quantum Energy System of every person is pure Cause and Effect.

Humankind has acquired power over the physical universe by acquiring the knowledge of its laws, codified as the physical sciences. The purpose of this book is to codify for you the knowledge of the laws of the Human Quantum Energy System, to introduce you to a non-physical science of Life. This knowledge will give you the power to control all these energies within you, and to help others (family, community and organization) to learn to control theirs. It will give you the power to permanently eliminate the Negative Human Energies from your organization, and to permanently increase the positive. As you will see later, eliminating negative energy is the most important factor in improving the Human Energy Climate (and therefore the productivity) of your organization. You cannot maintain and increase positive energy while there are negative energy leaks in the system.

The term Human Energy Climate defines the net combination of all the human mental, emotional, and behavioral energies, both positive and negative of an organization (business energy system). Positive human energy, which includes commitment, intelligence, initiative, creativity and good relationships with others, is the basis of smooth operations and high productivity of any organization. Negative Human Energy, which includes anger, resentment, hate, indifference, irresponsibility, personal aversions, among others, is the root cause of interpersonal frictions, problems, and errors that interfere with operations and therefore with production in both quality and quantity.

The Human Energy Climate can be felt as the overall morale, motivation, enthusiasm and job satisfaction in the organization. Look around you. What is the Human Energy Climate in your organization? What is the Human Energy climate of your family? Now look deeper still. What is the Human Energy Climate within you?

Summary:

- There are two kinds of energy in life: physical energies and the non-physical energies of mind, motivations and relationships and the deeper still, Human Quantum Energies of spirit itself.
- The Human Quantum Energies include: will, decision, determination, persistence, commitment, loyalty; all types of thought and mind processes, ideas, knowledge, intelligence, and creativity; the entire Emotional Energy polarity which includes joy, enthusiasm, indifference, anger, fear, hate, grief, depression—indeed all the emotions; and all causes of

behaviors, both in regards to communication and treatment; and things such as job performance.

- The Human Quantum Energies are more powerful than physical energies. They choose, motivate, and direct all human behavior and effort, both interactions with others and with things.

- The human being as a Quantum Energy System is the basic unit, the basic "chip" of all Organizational Energy Systems.

- The vast majority of the conflicts and problems in an organization are Negative Quantum Energy problems. Even most of the problems in the physical universe of the organization originate in Negative Human Quantum Energies.

- It is impossible to improve the Human Energy Climate and therefore the Power of an organization without substantially reducing and eventually eliminating the Negative Human Quantum Energy in the system.

Chapter 2

Polarity

M ost forms of energy are polarities. It is impossible to fully understand and control energy without understanding the laws that govern Polarity. A Polarity Spectrum is created by taking any unique energy and "stretching" it in two opposing directions, towards two extremes or poles. This creates a range or scale of variations of that particular energy, or experience, between the two poles. We call that range or scale a Polarity Spectrum.

For example, consider the Polarity Spectrum of temperature. Its two poles are hot and cold. The temperature of any thing in the physical universe can range from just above absolute zero at minus 459° F, the temperature of intergalactic space, (quite chilly, really) to about 100,000,000° F (sizzling) in the center of a supernova star.

A list of other Polarity Spectrums in the physical universe will make the concept of Polarity clear:

Light <> Dark

Big <> Little

Hard <> Soft

Sharp <> Dull

Pleasure <> Pain

Rich <> Poor

Health <> Sick

Profit <> Loss

The Color Spectrum

The Sound Spectrum

The Electromagnetic Radiation Frequency Spectrum

Spectrums are extremely important to existence, as they create an almost infinite variety of experience. Spectrums make life rich in possibilities and options. For example, how would life be if there were no hot or cold temperatures, no deserts, no snow, no winter or summer? How would life be if music did not exist because there was no sound spectrum? How grey would life be if the color spectrum did not exist?

However, here, we are not interested in physical energies or their Polarity Spectrums. We are interested in the non-physical energy spectrums. Here are a few of the Quantum Energy spectrums:

Powerful <> Powerless[5]

Cause <> Effect [6]

Knowledgeable <> Ignorant

Wise <> Foolish

Smart <> Stupid

Powerful <> Powerless

Strong <> Weak

Able <> Unable

Success <> Failure

Winner <> Loser

Valuable <> Worthless

Deserving <> Undeserving

Happiness <> UPS (Unhappiness, Pain[7] , Suffering)

Positive Emotions <> Negative Emotions

Good <> Bad

Acceptance <> Resistance

Affinity <> Aversion

Love <> Hate

Integration <> Separation

---

5 The symbols "<>" and " +/- ", (which mean positive / negative) in this book
will indicate that the term refers to a polarity. Examples: Happiness +/- will
refer to the Happiness <> Pain Polarity.
6 Cause <> Effect and Strong <> Weak are also physical spectrums, but here
they refer to quantum spectrums of these qualities in people.
7 "Pain" in this book will always mean mental or emotional pain, not physical
pain unless physical pain is specified. Happiness must be distinguished from
(physical) pleasure, and emotional pain distinguished from physical pain.

Marriage <> Divorce
Life <> Death

Look at these Polarity Spectrums and ask yourself: Do these Polarity Spectrums exist? Are they real? Do you experience them, feel them, in life? How dull would life be without these Polarity Spectrums? Could life even work without them? Are you trying to control these spectrums, to increase the positive sides in your life, and decrease the negative sides?

You will see that the ultimate motivation of everything you do in life is to control some of these polarities.

The Laws of Polarity:

There are several fundamental and important Laws of Polarity. The one shown in this chapter is so important that the failure to understand it guarantees unhappiness.

- Both poles of a polarity must exist.
- You can't have one pole without the other.

Corollary: You cannot have a spectrum without two poles. Any two points become poles and create a spectrum between them.

Corollary: You cannot have one side of a spectrum without the other side.

In other words, you can't have the positive of anything without the negative of it also existing. It is impossible for happiness to exist without pain; good without bad; success without failure; joy without sorrow. For any form of polar experience to exist, both poles, and therefore polarities, must exist. You cannot have one polarity without the other. Negatives must exist. To resist anything negative in life is to resist Life as it is and as it must be.

Resistance:

One of the laws of Quantum Energy is that Resistance Causes Persistence. Resistance is any Negative Energy sent against something considered negative to stop, change, punish, or destroy it. Forms of resistance energy include anger, fear, grief, and depression. We resist negative events, things others do or say that we don't like. We even resist ourselves, how we are; and we even resist our resistance energies when we resist being angry, fearful or depressed.

The use of Quantum Resistance Energy to stop or change anything is usually unsuccessful. Resistance energy just piles up against the Negative Energy it is supposed to stop or change so that the end result becomes twice as much Negative Energy. A very common example of this occurs when one person is angry (a Negative Energy) and starts blaming and invalidating (outputting Negative Energy) another person, who in turn gets angry and responds in kind. The result is two angry people. The more Negative Energy, resistance, they mutually throw against each other, the worse the relationship becomes. Thus, resistance makes what could have been just a flare-up, grow and solidify into lasting hate. Obviously, people resisting each other injects Negative Energy into your family, community and organizational Energy Climate. As communication and cooperation deteriorate, organizational power and production suffers.

All efforts to not feel your Negative Emotions are forms of

resistance. As to resisting your own Negative Emotions, that resistance in fact only causes their persistence and so increases your Negative Energy, or pain. The only pain that exists in life is your own Negative Emotions. It is never events[8], never what happens or what other people do or say that causes your experience of pain. This may seem strange and uncomfortable, but the mechanism by which your pain occurs will be shown in a later chapter. Therefore, when you resist your Negative Emotions, you are attempting to avoid pain by creating more pain.

Here is the point: Your Negative Emotions are your resistance energy to the negative things in life. Those things must exist! By the Laws of Polarity, negative experience must exist. Your resistance to negative experience only serves to cause its persistence and your pain. Furthermore, your pain is your emotional resistance, never the thing itself. It is your emotional resistance to the negative polarities in life, which is the only pain and unhappiness that exists.

You decide what to resist in life. Thus, you are the sole creator of all your unhappiness and pain in life! You create your pain by resisting the negatives polarities that must be as they are for the positive to exist. Thus, most people live resisting one entire side of Life, one half of Life, as it is and as it must be. And the kicker is that the negatives never cause your pain and unhappiness: only your resistance does! Again, if this seems impossible, just hold the thought. It will be shown later beyond all doubt.

---

8 Definition: "external event", or "events", or "externals": Any change or movement of anything external to you. It can mean any person, place, thing, occurrence, situation or circumstance. It can be anything anyone says or does, anything that happens, the arrival or departure of anybody or any thing. The word is used most generally to mean anything around you.

Remember:
 What Is, Is. What Ain't, Ain't.
 Unhappiness is never What Is.
 Unhappiness is your Resistance to What Is.

You can not successfully handle Negative Energy with Negative Energy because all you will create is more and more Negative Energy. Notice if this is what you have been doing with yourself, with your family, and with your organization. Have you been struggling to stop Negative Energy with Negative Energy with behaviors such as more and more rules, restrictive control mechanisms, anger, threats, punishments or other forms of Negative Energy? Hasn't worked, has it?

You need three things to handle and eliminate Negative Energy from yourself, another person, and from any Energy System such as your family, your department, your organization or your country. These three things are:

- Wisdom
- Response-ability
- SPace

The fact that Negative Energy must exist for Positive Energy to exist, does not mean that the Negative Energy must exist in your life or your organization. While there is no shortage of Negative Energy, you don't need to participate in it or contribute to it—and there is no way to be happy if you do so. We need to pause here and make a distinction between "negative" and "bad" as they are not at all the same.

Negative is that which is undesired, unpleasant or counter-productive. "Bad" is what should not be, thereby justifying the use of Negative Energy to destroy it. To clarify the difference between "bad" and "negative", consider this example: You want to go from New York to London, but by mistake get on the plane to Los Angeles. The plane to Los Angeles is not bad, but it is negative as it doesn't help you reach your objective—to get to London.

Negative Energy is not bad (should not be). On the contrary, it must be for the Positive Energy to exist. However, the fact that they must be, does not mean that you have to generate, partake, or contribute to them, or have them in your life or organization. Furthermore, you can not use Negative Energy to try to eliminate Negative Energy: that only causes resistance and persistence of the Negative Energy you want to eliminate. This is the Great Error that most people make: they try to eliminate Negative Energy with Negative Energy. That only piles up more Negative Energy.

For example, stop and recall the last time you exchanged angry words with another person. Your anger, your Negative Energy, was an attempt, through resistance, to control or stop Negative Energy from the other person. But what was the result? Did the other person respond in Negative Energy, perhaps anger, as resistance to your Negative Energy. Perhaps you succeeded in obtaining resignation or surrender from the other person, but this is yet another flavor or modulation of Negative Energy. Here both parties are experiencing Negative Emotion, as they struggle to end Negative Energy with Negative Energy. This is not "bad", but it is counterproductive, and therefore negative, to creating the happiness that you desire to experience.

Summary:

Life is Polarity; the play of opposites, and the play between opposites. Both poles must exist for either to exist. You cannot have positive without negative. Things can be negative without being bad.

Negatives must exist – but you, your family, and your organization do not have to live generating Negative Energy, or resisting it and therefore causing its persistence.

To resist negatives is to resist life as it is and must be. Your emotional resistance to the negatives of life that must be, is the only pain and suffering that exist. Your pain and suffering in life is never what happens, but your emotional resistance to what happens. Resistance is Negative Energy against Negative Energy and only causes the persistence of the negatives thus resisted. Whenever you resist Life you lose, always.

You can control and eliminate Negative Energy from your life and organization. But you cannot control the Negative Energy in you, in others, or in your organization by resisting it or by using Negative Energy against it.

CHAPTER 3

Negative Energy

Negative Energy is any energy that is painful, undesired, or counter-productive to your happiness or to your goals, and therefore to your power. Again, those characteristics do not make it bad energy, only negative. In the previous chapter it was shown that Negative Energy must exist for positive to exist. Since "Bad" is that which should not exist, our Negative Energies, therefore are not "Bad", just counter-productive to the positive experience that we wish to experience. By the Law of Polarity, these negative experiences must exist.

Although Negative Energy must exist, you do not have to operate with Negative Energy within you, your family, your community, or your organizations. By understanding how it is generated, as part of the Nuclear Energies of the human being, you can eliminate Negative Energy.

Technically, the concept of Negative Energy or a Negative Energy situation includes:

- Painful energy such as anger, fear, grief, depression
- Wrong kind of energy such as AC electrical current when you need DC current, or joviality when solemnity is appropriate
- Wrong polarity of energy: positive when you need negative, or negative when you need positive
- Counter-productive energy: energy that produces undesired effects
- Incorrect quantity of energy, too much or too little
- Insufficient quality (purity) of energy; has static or undesired peaks of frequency or amplitude
- Incorrectly timed energy, either too slow, too late; or too fast, too early

For the most part the above list identifies energy of the physical universe. Of major interest to you is the Negative Quantum Energies "inside" of people that cause Negative Energies and poor results in your life, groups and organizations. You are already quite familiar with such energies, and a simple list will suffice to make clear what Negative Energies are being referred to here.

Examples of Negative Human Quantum Energies:

Negative Emotion Energy
Frustration
Impatience
Hostility
Anger
Rage
Anxiety
Worry
Fear
Guilt
Resentment
Envy, Jealousy
Hate
Sorrow, Sadness, Loneliness
Desperation
Depression
Apathy

Negative Thoughts
Low Self-Esteem
Invalidations to Self and Others
Making Bad and Wrong
Blame and Guilt
Epithets
Victim Mentality
Dictator Mentality
Programs (All ideas of what should/should not be. Denial of freedom to be.)
Ego (All efforts to exalt oneself by debasing others; arrogance.)
Prejudices and Bigotry.
Masks: pretending to be what you are not.

Negative Actions and Behaviors
Blaming others
Negative Energy Communications
Not keeping your word, agreement, promises
Dishonesty, lying, stealing, embezzling
Addictions to tobacco, drugs, food, alcohol
Poor Management or Leadership; Micro Management
Retaliations, Revenge, Sabotage
Gossip and Rumors
Ego Power Struggles
Disloyal Ambition and Competition/ Misalignment of priorities

Negative Results
Discussed below

Life works according to a Causal Sequence that is

BE →FEEL →THINK →DO →HAVE

The Causal Sequence of Life is an ordered series of factors, each of which determines the nature of the following ones. Since your experience, indeed your life, functions according to this formula you must understand how it works. With this understanding you will be able to control, have power over your life. This formula will be examined in more depth later. The classifications of the Negative Human Energies from the previous lists apply to the Causal Sequence as follows:

1. **Negative Emotion Energy = FEEL:** All the negative, painful emotional energies.
2. **Negative Thoughts = THINK:** All forms of thought energy: ideas, desires, plans, goals, etc. Every thought is a thing, an object, made of mental frequency energy.
3. **Negative Actions & Behaviors = DO:** All behaviors, habits, actions, treatment of others, reactions to others actions, and communication.
4. **Results in Your Physical Universe = HAVE:** The results that show up in your life.

Some of these will overlap as, obviously, THINKing leads to DOing, and DOing leads to HAVEing or results. The negative FEEL → THINK → DO Energies above produce the following Negative HAVE (negative Results) for your organization and the people in it.

Negative HAVE:

The results of BE → FEEL → THINK → DO from the prior list of Negative Energies: The Negative Results in Your Organization

- Latent, simmering, and sometimes explosive emotional reactivity
- Some people on hair triggers, others cautious, defensive, fearful

- Interpersonal aversions, resistances, and conflicts.
- Arguments, quarreling, disputes resulting in strained relationships and reduced communications
- Jealousies, power and turf struggles
- Low morale and motivation, indifference, lethargy
- Reduced, slowed, withheld, and lost communications
- Reduced responsibility and Initiative
- Reduced creativity and resourcefulness
- Indifference to the mission and goals of the organization
- Poor compliance with safety and organizational policie.
- Mis-ordered or omitted priorities
- Tardiness and absenteeism
- Gossip and rumors
- Insecurity, lack of trust and confidence, fear
- Feelings of powerlessness, hopelessness and victim mentality
- Lack of cooperation and support between people and departments
- Unhappiness, emotional pain and suffering of the people in the workplace
- Retaliations and revenge
- Rebellion and sabotage
- Mistakes, omissions, errors, all leading to breakdowns
- Poor job satisfaction, resistance to working in your organization
- High general turnover, low retention
- Loss of your best people due to the Negative Energy

climate of the workplace
- Chaos in the organization. Poor departmental and poor overall performance and production
- Inattention and poor service leading to a loss of Customers

Does this list look familiar? You will recall that these are the symptoms of a dysfunctional organization introduced at the very start. Perhaps these symptoms even describe your organization. If so, your business is not operating at full potential. Your negative organizational results are the consequence of operating within a negative Causal Sequence. All of the above increases costs and reduces profitability, and makes life unpleasant for all.

Do these Negative Energies exist? Do you sometimes experience them? Do you see them around you? What is the effect on your performance in particular, and the performance and production of your organization of such Negative Energies?

Observe this: in your organization, machines break down, products don't meet quality standards, supplies arrive late or are the wrong item, etc. These are situations that are of the physical universe. But notice that the vast majority of your problems are due to Negative Human Energy – Quantum, non-physical universe problems. Take note that many of the physical problems of your organization, are caused, or not corrected adequately, by people operating with Negative Energy.

The vast majority of problems and poor performance in organizations are caused by Negative Human Quantum Energy in the system. Problems with things and machines are relatively simple to solve. It is impossible to substantially and permanently improve your organization's performance, productivity, competitive edge, and profitability without reducing the Negative Quantum Energy in the organization.

To improve the Energy System that is your life, your family, and your organization, you must reduce to the minimum the Negative Human Energies in the system.

This is quite possible to do. All energies, Human Quantum Energies included, obey exact laws and principles. There is nothing accidental or random about Negative Human Energy. It has exact causes and precise remedies. Until now, no one has been able to solve the problem of Negative Human Quantum Energy.

It has not been solved by training, motivation, inspiration, or psychology. Businesses spend millions of dollars each year sending employees to training designed to inspire and motivate change and yet, employees (and therefore organizations) continue to be plagued by poor morale, a lack of fulfillment and reduced productivity.

Negative Human Energy continues to exist in your life because you have not identified the root cause of Negative Human Energy. As you progress through the pages ahead not only will you discover the exact causes of Negative Energy but you will learn that there is a way to create the Positive Energy that is your power in life.

SABOTAGE:

When people are in Negative Energy, they usually go into the condition of sabotage. We use the word sabotage with a special definition. It is not just actively damaging an energy system. The condition of sabotage exists any time a person is doing less than his or her best, less than 100% contribution, be it to the organization, a group, a relationship, or to oneself. Studying the following diagram will help to make the concept of sabotage clear:

FEEL and DO ENERGY LEVELS of People in an Energy System.

Relationship, Family, Group, Organization

BE→FEEL →THINK → DO → HAVE
FEEL motivates DO

FEEL	DO
Emotional Energy Level	Behavior and Action Energies
Passion	100% at Cause; doing one's best. Enthusiasm
Enthusiasm	Contribution at 99% or less of capability
Satisfaction	Participation
Contentment	Cooperation
Indifference	Indifference, neither support nor opposition
Hostility	Actively withholds positive energy and support but does not actively attack unless attacked.
Anger	Acts to damage or destroy in the heat of emotional charge.
Fear	Will not act openly. Uses covert, sporadic, or opportunistic efforts to damage or destroy.
Resentment and Hate (degrees of hardened, permanent anger)	Avowed Enemy: Openly committed to damage and destruction.
	Covert Enemy: Hides True Identity and intentions while working from without to damage or destroy.
	Treason and Traitor: Pretending to be ally while working from the inside to damage and destroy.
Grief	Too overwhelmed by negative energy to do much of anything, positive or negative, for the moment.
Apathy, Depression	Too little energy to do much of anything, positive or negative.

Sabotage HERE DOWN

58

Is anyone you know operating in sabotage in any group of which you are a part (coupleship, family, team, organization)?

Are you operating in sabotage in any group of which you are a part?

The General Cause of Negative Human Quantum Energy:

Why do people generate so much Negative Energy?

Frustration, hostility, anger, impatience, anxiety, fear, road rage, desk rage, worry, guilt, resentment, hate, sorrow, loneliness, sadness, grief, desperation, depression, and more – our lives seem to have no end of Negative Emotional Energy. Because life works BE → FEEL → THINK → DO → HAVE, that Negative Emotional Energy (negative FEEL) then generates negative thinking and negative behaviors. In other words, all negative behaviors and relationship conflicts originate in negative FEELings (anger, fear, guilt, resentment, hate, loneliness, depression, etc.).

By the Laws of Polarity, we have seen that Negative Energy must exist for the positives to exist. Therefore the experiences of love, happiness, joy, enthusiasm, for example, could not exist if their opposites did not exist. However, no Energy System operates well with negative energies. Negative Energy is, by definition, that which is counter-productive or harmful to the Energy System. Some systems are designed to handle, filter out, or operate in spite of negative energies, but nobody designs a system itself to run on Negative Energy. This is also true of the human being. We were not designed to run on Negative Emotional Energy, and it is painful and counter-happiness to do so. In fact, the instinct to avoid or escape Negative Energy while not knowing how leads us into the trap of our resisting our own and other's Negative Energies. It is this resistance which causes pain and the persistence of what is resisted.

Computer Analogy:

To understand the general cause of Negative Human Energy, consider your computer. The basic software of a computer is called the operating system. The operating system is a general program that tells all the rest of the computer how to function and behave. Examples of operating systems include Microsoft Windows 3, 95, 98, 2000, XP and Vista; Linux, DOS, MAC, and UNIX. Once the operating system is installed and working you can install other programs called applications on top of the operating system. However, the operating system is the basic control system; it controls both the hardware and the applications.

There is a law in computation known as GIGO— Garbage In, Garbage Out. It means that if your program input to the computer system has errors in it (garbage), you will get errors (garbage) out of the system. As an operating system consists of many thousands, even hundreds of thousands of lines of code, errors and flaws, "garbage programming" is common. Anybody with even minimum experience of Windows and its constant updates to correct flaws has lived this. If you have used a computer much, you remember how the earlier versions of Windows were plagued with the famous "blue screen of death", indicating that you had to reboot the system.[9] You have also probably heard of, if not personally experienced, what viruses, spyware, worms, and

---

9   Windows XP still does this, but now Windows reboots itself automatically without having to reboot the hardware. You will see it do this when the entire screen goes blank and then comes back on, often with the problem application closed.

trojans can do to a computer. All of these are different forms of negative energies in the computer system and all produce conflicts, problems, and stoppages.

People work very much the same way. They have an operating system in their being and mind, and it has flaws and "garbage". Every human being has a set of fundamental ideas about how life works. The Human Operating System (HOS) includes ideas, beliefs, and values about many things, including self, others, love, happiness, family, relationships, money, and work. The HOS also is the seat of self-image, self-esteem, character, and personality among other things. It is a data bank that holds our rules and programs of how to operate our life, including our internal energies such as thought, emotions, and our dealings, communications, and reactions to others.

Human Operating Systems around the world have many basic, "lines of code" shared by almost all people. For example, the vast majority of us put a high value on money and family. However, there are also great differences. You can see these differences by studying different cultures, as each culture has its unique code. An American, a Jordanian, a Mexican, a Russian, will all sometimes behave very differently in the same situation. These differences in both feeling and behaviors have been "programmed" into them— into their operating system since childhood.

All of our Negative Emotions, negative thinking, behaviors, and relationship conflicts occur because of GIGO: we have garbage in our HOS. We suffer in life because of major errors, flaws, and viruses in our basic programming of how life works, of how our mental, emotional, and relationship energies work. Life and human beings are not designed and do not need to operate with Negative Energy. Negative Energy only exists because of flaws in our programming. It is not built into the human being as necessary. It must exist for the positive to exist, but the human being does not have to generate Negative Energy and only does so because of programming, HOS errors. It is that simple. Negative Human Quantum Energy is the result of flaws, glitches, viruses, and worms –garbage—in the operating system, in the programming of the person generating that Negative Energy. GIGO.

Repair the programming by updating the HOS and you eliminate the flaws and viruses that cause the generation of the Negative Energy. The entire Quantum Energy system of that person then begins to function as it should, with all Positive Energies. This is what this book introduces: the HOS update that needs to be installed in all persons so the Quantum operating system functions correctly, according to the laws of Energy and Life.

People do not generate Negative Energy because they want to. Negative Energy is painful for them and for those around them, including the people that they love, such as their spouse, children and family. Negative Energy prevents people from experiencing their full potential which has a negative impact on your organization.

People generate Negative Energy because their HOS is deficient. They don't understand how Quantum Energy works, and how to control it. They generate Negative Energy because they do not know how Energy, their being, and Life operate. They know more about computers than they do about themselves. Knowledge is Power, and they not only do not have the right knowledge about their internal energies, but they have inaccuracies, flaws, garbage, in their knowledge, in their programming.

This lack of knowledge is so extensive that most people not

only do not know how to control it; they don't even know that they can control it. And it gets worse: most people believe that they can't control their energies such as their emotions, for example, and think that their energies are controlled by external events such as other people, things or situations. As a result, they take their Negative Energy and attack external events and those around them to try to stop or change them. Obviously, this injects Negative Energy into the Group Energy Systems. These beliefs are one of the prime viruses in the current, obsolete HOS. Correcting these erroneous beliefs is a basic and important part of the new HOS.

CHAPTER 4

The New Human Operating System

How Life Really Works

The Causal Sequence in depth:

Your life functions according to a Causal Sequence whether you know it or not, and whether you want it to or not. There is no escaping it: it controls your existence. You can only learn how the Sequence works and harness it to your benefit. Doing so will give you great power over life.

The Causal Sequence is:

BE →FEEL → THINK → RELATE / DO → HAVE

The Causal Sequence can also be expressed as:

Here each element in the second statement of the sequence is equivalent to the corresponding element in the first statement. "RELATE" refers to dealings with others and includes communication, one's treatment of others, and one's reactions to others' treatment of oneself.

The Causal Sequence works like this:

Who I AM (BE) determines
  What I FEEL which determines
    How I THINK which determines my
      RELATE: How I communicate & treat others, and
        How I ACT, BEHAVE. My ACTIONS determine
          My <u>Results = HAVE</u> in life.

Laws relevant to the Causal Sequence include:

- Everything in your life falls into one of these six areas. It is life itself.
- It is a Causal Sequence because each element determines the following ones.
- Your life consists of your Causal Sequences. Everything in your life is part of a Causal Sequence.

- The beauty of the Causal Sequence is that you only need to learn to control the first element, your BEing, to control all the rest of your life.

When referring to any element of the Causal Sequence, it will be capitalized to make sure the reader knows that it refers to the Sequence.

Examples of words that will be capitalized include: BE, BEing, FEEL, FEELing, FELT, DO, DOing, DID, SAY, SAYing, RELATEing, RELATIONships, HAVEing, HAD, etc.

Here is a more detailed explanation of what each element covers:

HAVE = RESULTS:

Your HAVE is everything material that shows up in your life, the good and the bad. It does not matter whether you take responsibility for it being there or not; if it exists in your life, it is part of your HAVE. It is your "fame and fortune" in the world. Your HAVE includes all your material possessions and properties. It includes your business, job, and career; your money, bank accounts and financial condition. It includes your successes and your failures. It includes the quantity and quality of your relationships (but not the actions you take to create those results; that would be your DO). It includes your body and its condition of health or sickness. It includes all events, everything that happens to you, whether you call it luck, coincidence, or accident. If it occurs in your life; you HAVE it.

Negative HAVE: Everything in your life that you have but don't want and have not been able to eliminate. Examples can include a health problem, an accident, insufficient money, debts, a job you dislike, conflictive relationships.

Your Not-HAVE: Everything you do want but have not been able to manifest, for example, a better job, more money, a new house, a satisfying relationship.

DO= ACTIONS and BEHAVIORS: The concept of DO in the Causal Sequence includes all your actions, habits, customs, and behaviors. You have two basic areas of DO: people and things.

Your RELATE: This is your DO, your actions and behaviors, in regards to other people. Your RELATE includes how you communicate, deal with, treat, act and interact with others. It includes how you react to their treatment of you.

Your DO with things: Includes how you perform your work or business activities. It includes your driving ability, your ability to use a computer, hobbies, and anything else you do in life.

Your Negative DO: Everything that you DO and want to stop DOing or know you should stop DOing, but the behavior continues. This can include bad habits, substance abuse, and addictions, as well as compulsions, aversions, and obsessions.

Your Not DO: Anything that you want to do or know that you should do, but you have not taken action to accomplish. Common examples of Not DO include leaving the nest, changing jobs or careers, moving to another city, getting married, or getting divorced.

Your Positive DO: Keeping your word, being on time, listening attentively, working with quality, driving carefully, working to the best of your ability, acting with responsibility and accountability.

Your Negative DO: Includes such behaviors as criticizing, arguing, blaming, procrastinating, being late, laziness, not communicating, giving the silent treatment, being stubborn, complaining, smoking, overeating, taking drugs, arriving late.

THINK = THOUGHT = MIND: Your THINK is everything that occurs or exists in your mind. There are two parts to this:

1. The thoughts, which are thought-energy objects;
2. The processes and activities of thinking.

Your varieties of thought-energy creations include: ideas, concepts, desires, goals, plans, dreams, memories, knowledge, data, information, values, beliefs, dogmas, programs, paradigms, and visions. Your THINK includes all the content of your subconscious and your unconscious.

Your THINK is the creation and manipulation of thought objects. Your THINKing processes and activities include: analyzing, comparing, deciding, imagining, remembering, memorizing, visualizing, creativity, design and creation, intuition, and planning. All of your DO in the mind is considered THINK.

FEEL = EMOTION: Your FEEL includes all your feelings and emotions, both positive and negative. Your FEELings include: love, joy, enthusiasm, rejoicing, interest, delight, affection, attraction, aversion, anger, fear, anxiety, panic, phobia, worry, guilt, resentment, hate, sadness, sorrow, depression, grief, mourning, regret, apathy, and any other sentiment of any kind.

BE = IDENTITIES

Your IDentities are your creations of self, of who you are, or who you are not. Most of them are declarations of "I am", or "I am not". Your creations of your Self are subtle energies, but they are the most powerful things in your life. They begin and determine your Causal Sequences, and therefore all the other aspects of your life. BEing will be discussed in greater detail.

Notice that of the six arenas, only two are in the physical universe: DO with things, and HAVE. The other four are Quantum: BE, FEEL, THINK, and RELATE.

Also note that the most important things in life are Quantum Energies. This includes who you are, how you FEEL (both your painful emotions and your Positive Emotions), your experience of love and happiness, the quality of your relationships, your knowledge, learning ability, intelligence, intuition, and creativity – all are Quantum Energies.

Quantum Energies are more powerful and more important than physical energies. Quantum Energies determine and control physical energies. Now that you have been introduced to the players, the six elements of the causal sequence, you will learn how they interact to create your organization, and more importantly, your life.

Just as everything in the physical universe (your external world) obeys exact laws, so does everything in your non-physical or Quantum universe (your internal world) obey exact laws. There is nothing random or chaotic about either universe. In both universes, Knowledge is Power, the power to control and produce the desired results.

THINK → RELATE / DO → HAVE

Understanding THINK → RELATE / DO → HAVE is easy, as it is fairly obvious that life does work according to this part of the Causal Sequence. Your THINKing includes everything in your mind, conscious and unconscious. It includes your intelligence, intuition, analytical abilities and creativity. It includes what you have learned, your knowledge, your memories, your past experiences, your reasoning processes, and therefore your wisdom. Obviously, you THINK to decide what actions to take, with both people (RELATE) and things (DO). Once you have selected what to DO, you then apply your knowledge, ideas, and creativity to direct and guide your actions to produce the results, the HAVE, that you desire. Thus, THINK is both what to do and how to do it.

For example, your THINKing at work, your knowledge, training, intelligence, and creativity determine how well you perform, how well you DO, on the job. Your performance, at least theoretically, determines how much you earn (HAVE in the form of money), which in turn determines the material abundance in which you live (more HAVE).

Thus, we have THINK → RELATE / DO → HAVE or simply THINK → DO → HAVE, for short.

Be careful not to underrate the importance of RELATE. RELATE, which includes communication and all interactions with others, is especially important to leaders, managers, and supervisors, because their job is to get the work done through the training and motivation of others. Communication, education, training, and motivation are constant and continual RELATE activities for a leader.

There are other important concepts related to THINK → DO → HAVE, including Power.

Power is the ability to act and perform correctly (DO) to produce the desired results (HAVE).

Therefore: THINK is the mother of <u>Power = DO →</u> <u>HAVE</u>

Power comes from knowledge. Knowledge guides actions to produce the desired results, which is the definition of power. Therefore we have the famous saying, Knowledge Is Power. Knowledge is correct THINK; therefore THINK → Power.

A corollary of these laws is:

The cause of conflicts, problems, and failures in life is the lack of the correct knowledge.

As you proceed through this book you will see very clearly that erroneous THINK is at the root of all problems in life. The HOS is a THINK. It is the subconscious and erroneous THINK that is guiding people's actions (DO), including their inability to stop or control their generation of Negative Energies (FEEL) that are painful to themselves and others. The Negative Human Energies are the principle hindrance to the optimum performance of your organization. This book is about a new THINK, a new Human Operating System that fixes the erroneous THINK → DO → HAVE sequence. Unfortunately, very few people understand and apply these laws, Knowledge Is Power and THINK→ DO→ HAVE. Very few people understand that the cause of their conflicts, problems and failures in life is their own lack of the correct knowledge. They are ignorant of the importance and effects of their own Causal Sequence, their own THINK→ DO→ HAVE, on their lives.

Ignorant of these laws, most people, when they have conflicts and problems, look outside of themselves and see others as the cause of their conflicts and problems. They blame and attack others with Negative Energy as the apparent cause of their problems and pain, trying to "fix" others to remedy their emotional problems. This is the source of most of the Negative Quantum Energy in your organization. The real cause of conflicts and problems with others is a lack of the knowledge necessary to communicate and negotiate with others, a lack of how RELATE works. Likewise, the real cause of their Negative Emotions is their own lack of the right knowledge of what their emotions are and how they really work. This is the subject of the next chapter.

FEEL

The Causal Sequence of Life is:

BE → FEEL → THINK → DO → HAVE.

In the previous section you learned that THINK → DO → HAVE leads to power (or lack of). The Causal Sequence shows that FEEL precedes THINK, that FEEL determines THINK. This, at first, may seem strange. Most people think that their THINKing determines how they FEEL. This is not so, and is one of the erroneous ideas that we want to correct with the new HOS (Human operating system). FEELing comes before and determines THINKing, not the other way around. People DO and try to HAVE what they THINK will make them happy, make them FEEL good. They use their THINK to try to DO → HAVE what they THINK will make them FEEL happy. FEEL rules THINK, not the other way around. However, people live trying to work the Causal Sequence backwards. One of the errors of THINK here is to think that anything external will ever control your emotions and keep you happy.

People THINK → DO → HAVE in order to FEEL good, to be happy.

Law: The ultimate motivation of all human behavior and effort (THINK, DO and HAVE) is one's own happiness.

This law is called the Existential Imperative. It rules humanity. It is, simply put, the drive to be happy that is within each of us, and is the most powerful drive we have. Psychology calls it the Pleasure—Pain Principle, but it is much more than that. For one thing, pleasure is physical while happiness is a Quantum Energy; it is non-physical. Likewise there is physical pain and Quantum or Emotional pain. You can even be opposite polarities of these at the same time. For example, imagine you just won a tough game of football; you are all bruised and aching, but joyous. Another example is childbirth. While experiencing tremendous pain, mothers are happy as they go through the event. As you proceed through this book you will learn different ways that this Existential Imperative expresses itself in our feelings, thoughts and actions.

Does the Existential Imperative, the drive to happiness as the ultimate motivation of all human behavior, seem true to you, or does it conflict with your current beliefs about life? If it conflicts, great! That means it is time to sit up and pay attention, because you are looking at the limits of your current Human Operating System. You have found missing or erroneous programming. That happiness is the ultimate motivation of all human actions is provable for any and all behavior. There are no exceptions to this law.

If you wish to prove it for yourself, look at anything you do, or have ever done, from your point of view of what you were THINKing at the moment of action. Compare who you thought you would BE and FEEL if you did not do that action, with who you wanted to BE and how you thought you would FEEL by doing that action, you will find that you always acted according to what you THOUGHT would give you the best IDentity (BE)[10] and the best FEEL. If you THINK you acted that way to make somebody else happy, observe that making somebody else happy is what you THOUGHT would make you happy. You made them happy to make yourself happy. In the final analysis, the ultimate motivation of your actions was your own happiness. This is true for every person, in every action they take.

Be clear here—this does not mean that our choices always work to bring us happiness, only that the criteria of our decisions *at the moment of action,* given what we knew at that time, was our happiness. Often times our choices backfire and we end up with problems and are less happy. However, consciously or subconsciously, we always DO what we THINK will make us FEEL happy. It will often be a win-win so that others are happy also, but the happiness of others is not our prime decision criteria: our own happiness is. Many people use "making others happy" a justification for their decisions and actions, but that is always a delusion. A familiar example is the parent who spoils her children. She will tell you she wants her children to be happy, to have things and opportunities that she never had. A deeper analysis

---

10 The concept of BE and IDentity may not be clear here as we do not cover this until the next chapter. If so, ignore them and just focus on your FEELing.

will show that there is a deeper meaning to her actions. She seeks to be happy by making her children happy, but when all is said and done, it is the mother's own happiness that is key.

You may be asking why is this important in a book about organizational power and success? It is important because you as the leader, manager, or supervisor need to profoundly understand, that happiness is the ultimate motivation of all your people and of everything that they do—including all their Negative Energies and negative behaviors. Their intention is always for their happiness, not yours, not the well-being of the company. What you have to do is restructure their HOS so that they are happy and align their happiness with the well-being of the company. You must reprogram their HOS (and yours) so that they have the power to be happy. That power is a result of the right knowledge.

To the degree that your employees are happy, they will happily contribute their best Positive Energy to the organization.

To the degree that your employees are unhappy, they will express that unhappiness in the form of Negative Energy, injecting it into the energy system that is your organization. Only unhappy people generate Negative Energy.

What percentage of the people in your organization are happy and what percentage are unhappy, expressing emotions such as hostility anger, resentment, spite, jealousy, fear, indifference, apathy, frustration, impatience, depression? In other words, happiness is the controlling energy in a human being. Not THINKing, not DOing, not HAVEing, but FEELing is what controls every person. And how a person FEELs will determine whether they generate and output Positive or Negative Energy. Unhappy people generate Negative Energy. To eliminate Negative Energy, conflicts and problems, and increase the productivity of your organization, you must understand how people FEEL. You must have happy people working in your organization.

Here you have a paradox sitting between the horns of a dilemma. You cannot control how other people FEEL. You may not even be able to control how you FEEL as yet. You can not make another person happy, including your spouse, your parents, or your children. It is impossible to make another person happy. The best you can do is give them a MOP, a Moment of Pleasure. MOPs are not true happiness; they are always fleeting and soon pass away.

Not only can you not control how other people FEEL or make them happy; you have no responsibility to even try to please others, make them happy, including your employees. The dilemma is that at the same time that you have no power to control their FEEL, you must have them become happy or you cannot improve the Energy Climate, and therefore the power in your organization.

In the past, if you have tried to do much for the motivation and happiness of your employees, you have tried to do so with changes in management policies, rewards and recognitions. These are the manipulation of external things trying to produce happiness, which is internal. Such efforts in the long run can only give mediocre results at best. If you want spectacular and permanent results, reprogram their HOS so that they can do it for themselves internally. Every human being is motivated to be happy–they just don't know how. The most powerful thing you can do as manager is to learn how to control your own FEELings and in turn, teach others how to control their own FEELings. By doing so, everyone becomes response-able creators of their own happiness. When you understand this, you will understand what others need to know to achieve the same power. Therefore, you are well served to understand the nature of FEELing and happiness, to be examined in the next chapter.

CHAPTER 5

Happiness

Law of Happiness:

Happiness is how you FEEL, and only how you FEEL. Happiness is purely a positive FEELing.

As your primary FEELings are your emotions, Happiness is purely emotional, the Positive Emotions. The opposite polarity of Happiness is Unhappiness, Pain & Suffering (UPS). UPS is likewise, purely emotional; it is the Negative Emotions. Remembering that "pain" refers to emotional pain, this can be restated with a simple formula:

Positive Emotions = Happiness
Negative Emotions = UPS (Unhappiness, Pain & Suffering)

Check this law by trying to find any event[11] in your life that was happy or unhappy other than by your FEELings, your emotions, in relation to that event. Also note that other people that experienced that same event may have FELT very differently. You may have been happy, and they sad; or vice versa, they FELT happy, and you FELT sad.

Two very simple examples of this could be:

1) Someone that you like, that someone else dislikes.
2) A promotion that someone received at work and about which you were glad, while others were mad and vice versa.

In both cases, it is the same external event, yet two totally different emotional responses. This, as we shall see shortly, shows that external events do not cause internal emotional experience. The Happiness <> UPS Polarity and the Emotional Energy -/+ Polarity are exactly the same Energies, as shown in the following equation:

Emotion Polarity Spectrum = Happiness Polarity Spectrum

Emotions are not random, neither in "flavor" or in cause. They have an exact order to them. There are exact causes of the

---

11 Remember the definition of "event": "external event", or "events", or "externals". Any change or movement of anything external to you. It can mean any person, place, thing, occurrence, situation or circumstance. It can be anything anyone says or does, anything that happens, the arrival or departure of anybody or anything. The word is used most generally to mean anything around you.

emotions and of which particular emotion a person experiences at any time. This will be explained in detail in the next chapter.

The following diagram illustrates the Emotion Polarity Spectrum:

Polarity Spectrum of the Emotions
(Only the main ones are shown)

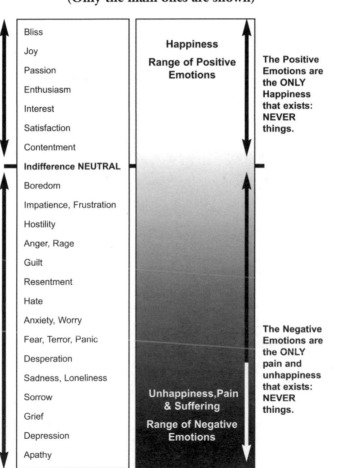

Law: Your emotions are never caused by external events.

Your happiness, your emotional pain, are never caused by what happens, by other people, situations, or things. In the physical universe we can observe that physical events do cause physical experience. For example: under normal circumstances—sugar, salt, fire, and ice all cause the same physical experience to everybody, everywhere, every time they are applied. There is consistency of cause and effect. Thus, there is a true Cause-Effect relationship between physical events and our physical experience.

However, when we observe Quantum experience, this is never true. For any given external event, we find that Human Quantum experience such as thoughts, opinions, judgments, and FEELings, is completely variable. If we hold constant an external event but observe a variety of human thoughts and emotions about that event, then the cause of the variations must be within that which is varying, the people, and not that which is constant, the event. There is no other possibility. There is no cause effect relationship between external events and human Quantum experiences.

This means that every person is the cause, the creator, of their Quantum experience, of their thoughts and emotions, of their THINKing and FEELing. The absence of this datum is, in fact, one of the primary errors of the old HOS. The illusion that external events cause the emotions, our Happiness <> Pain, is the cause of untold misery in our lives, and of most of the conflicts and problems in your organization, your family and the world. Very few people understand that they are the creators of their experience. The consequences of that ignorance are enormous, for self and for others.

One of the first consequences is that as long as a person

82

is ignorant of the fact that he is the creator of his Quantum experience, it will be impossible for him to ever be much happier than he is right now; which for most of humanity is more unhappy than happy. The consequences for an organization are likewise enormous. As long as the people in the organization do not know that they are the creators of their emotions, of their happiness or their pain, there is no way to stop the generation of Negative Energy. Here is why.

When people live believing that external events cause their emotions they go into THINK → DO → HAVE. They scheme (THINK) trying to control (DO) external events (HAVE) in order to control their FEEL, to stop pain and be happy. We have just proved that this is impossible! It will never work; it can never work.

1) First, nobody has the power to control external events sufficiently to avoid negative events and produce only positive events. For example, the president of the United States is supposedly the most powerful person on earth and even s/he cannot control most events either at home or abroad.

2) Secondly, external events do not determine your FEELings, your emotions. Therefore, no amount of control, or accumulation of material things, will ever produce happiness. Do you believe that a person with $1 million a year income is necessarily happier than a person with $50,000 a year income? Do you know anyone who has achieved significant financial success and yet remains unhappy? Even "getting it all" is no guarantee of happiness. There

are lots of people who "have it all" and yet are unhappy, known for failed relationships and substance
abuse. The list of movie, sports, and music celebri-
ties is filled with the names of highly successful, yet
unhappy people.

The problem is further exacerbated as people try to control
external events, usually with Negative Energy. Moreover, they
overstep the boundaries of liberty and try to control the BE,
THINK and DO of other people and do so with Negative Energy. This is a denial of freedom and of every person's right to
create one's life. Trying to dictate to others what they should
or should not do will almost always meet with resistance and
counter-attack. It is this projection of Negative Energy to control events that injects the internal Negative Energies of people
into the organizational Energy System. People take their internal
Negative Energies such as anger, resentment, jealousy, ambition,
hate, desires for retaliation and revenge and either discharge and
dump them on others, or hide them and go into sabotage.

It is impossible to control your emotions by controlling external events; the best you can do is a MOP[12] and these always
pass. However, as long as people do not understand this, they
will continue to attack externals, including their superiors and
the organization itself, as the *apparent* cause of their Negative
Emotions, and as the entity *apparently* responsible for making

---

12 MOP: Moment of Pleasure: The fleeting high we get when we get our way
or achieve something. People waste their lives pursuing MOPs as a mirage of
happiness— Nothing external can ever maintain the internal positive emotional
state that is happiness.

them happy and failing to do so. This is what is going on in your organization; this is why there are so many unhappy people and so much Negative Energy hindering the organization.

If everyone in your organization truly understood just this one concept, **Responsibility for Experience**, that they are the Creators of their emotions, it would transform the Energy Climate. People would stop blaming others for how they FEEL and start to look inside and take control of their emotions. They would understand that there is no sense in and no need to attack and try to change others to control their emotions. You would begin to have SPace in the organization, allowing others to BE as they are, and not BE as they are not. This does not mean that you do not work to change events to how you want them to BE, only that you do not attack what is already packed with Negative Energy.

Currently, the people in your organization are looking to others, to you as management, and to the organization to make them happy, or at least to avoid activating their Negative Emotions and so "make" them suffer. Thus, they are trapped in the impossible dream of externally-caused happiness. There is no way that you or the organization can ever make them happy. Nor do you have any responsibility to do so.

As long as they are operating in the illusion that external things—you, management, the organization—*do* cause their emotions, *do* cause their pain, and *should* make them happy, they will continue to generate and attack you with Negative Energy. Although it should be obvious that attacking the world with Negative Energy is not a workable strategy for happiness, people never seem to tire of it. People simply do not seem to realize that their own Negative Emotional Energy is the only pain and suffering that exists, and that the first person to feel that Negative Energy is the person generating it. Thus each person is the sole source of his or her unhappiness in life. If this is still not real for you, not to worry. It will be covered in more depth, yet to come.

The first step in removing Negative Energy from your organization is to take a look at your own energies. In the same way that you are not responsible for the happiness of your employees, others and the organization are not responsible for your happiness. They do not cause your emotions, your anger, your frustration or your happiness—on the job or off the job. To be happy, you must take control of your emotions and create your own happiness no matter the events around you. Life will always be a parade of events. If your happiness depends on only positive events, or on you controlling those events, there would be no hope for your happiness, or that of any person. Fortunately, happiness does not work that way.

Your control of your internal Energies (identities, emotions and thoughts) is the only way you can ever achieve and maintain true happiness— happiness which is the Imperative of life. And only *you* can do it; only you can take control of your emotions. Nor can you control the emotions or happiness of others. For success, it is essential to reduce the Negative Energy in your organization. You can't control their energies, but you can begin to take control of your energies and provide your employees with a valuable learning opportunity. Only when you and every person in the organization, takes responsibility for their energies can each begin to control them, and only when everyone begins to control them, will the Negative Human Quantum Energy in your organization be reduced. This will make life much easier and more pleasant for you and for everyone. With this reduction in Negative Energy businesses and organizations achieve true power to accomplish their goals and objectives.

In every situation, there are two separate sides. The first side is the external event, circumstance, incident or person. The other side is your experience, your FEELings, your emotions. The first side never causes the second one. Events never cause your emotions.

You have, therefore, two separate situations to resolve:

1) The first one is your experience, particularly your emotions. You must learn to stop your Negative Emotions and remain in serenity, peace and happiness.

2) The second problem is handling the external event – and many times there will not be much that you can do. However, to be happy, you only need to handle your Negative Emotions, not the external event. Never confuse these two things.

Two Very Different Situations:

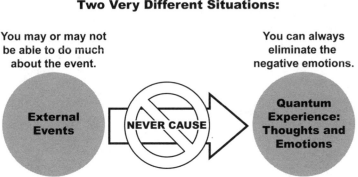

You may or may not be able to do much about the event.

You can always eliminate the negative emotions.

External Events

NEVER CAUSE

Quantum Experience: Thoughts and Emotions

Our next question is: Given that nothing outside of ourselves causes our emotions, what does cause them? What is it within us that generates our emotions, positive and negative, and therefore determines our Happiness or our Pain in life? Stay tuned. You've asked a great question.

Summary:

The Existential Imperative of Life is happiness. One's happiness is the Ultimate Motivation of all effort and behavior, of all THINK, RELATE, DO and HAVE.

Happiness is how you FEEL; it is purely emotional. Happiness is any experiential state of Positive Emotions. Negative Emotions are the only pain and suffering that exist in life.

Happiness is never the events in your Life, but how you FEEL in relation to those events. Furthermore, events are never the cause of your FEELings, of your emotions. Events never cause your pain and suffering in life; and events can never give you more than a most fleeting flash of happiness (a MOP).

To stop the generation of Negative Human Energy in an organization, people must first come to understand that nothing external to them ever causes their emotions, ever causes their pain.

Only then will they begin to look within to find the real causes and to free themselves of the compulsion to try to control the external world by attacking it with Negative Energy whenever it appears to have caused them pain.

What Is, Is. What Ain't, Ain't
Unhappiness, pain and suffering is never What Is, But rather

your emotional resistance to What Is, to Reality.

- You are the sole Creator of your resistance to Reality.
- Once something Is; It already Is As It Is.
- It is foolish to resist Reality with Negative Energy— that is your only pain in life.
- You can not create what you want, while resisting what you have.
- Wisdom focuses Positive Energy on creating the desired future Reality.
- The Positive Emotions are the only Happiness that exists; never people, things or events.
- The Negative Emotions are the only pain & suffering that exists; never people, things or events.

This is great news! Because if you had to control externals to be happy, there would be no hope for your happiness – nobody has the power to control other people or most of the events in their lives. Fortunately, to be happy all the time no matter what, you don't have to control events, only your emotions. This is relatively easy.

CHAPTER 6

The Nuclear Energy of Life

So far it has been shown that:

1) Happiness is the ultimate motivation of all human behavior and that
2) Happiness <> Pain is purely emotional; and that
3) Your Emotions +/- are never caused by external events; therefore
4) The causes of your Emotions are within you.

One of the great questions of life:

Exactly what is it within you that does cause your emotions?

Looking at the Causal Sequence:

BE → FEEL → THINK → DO → HAVE

We can see that it is BE, which means what you are BEing at any moment. As your emotions, FEELings, are constantly changing; we can know that your BEing must be constantly changing to cause your changes of emotions. So the question is: Just what is BE and BEing?

Shakespeare in Hamlet says, "To be or not to be; that is the question". However, that is not the question. You are always BEing and you cannot Not-BE. The question is WHAT are you BEing? To understand BEing, we must return to our basic concept of energy. Everything that exists is energy, including you, your BEing.

Observing the universe, we can see that energy moves in two opposing "direction". Thus, we are looking at yet another Polarity. These are known in thermodynamics as "ectropy" and "entropy", which we can call "up" and "down" respectively.

- Ectropy is the intelligent, causal, organizing force that combines materials and synergizes energy to create ever more powerful systems. It organizes and builds and heats things "up". Another name for ectropy is Life. Individual life forms are BEings.

- Entropy is the decaying force that tries to pull everything "down" to inert, homogenous matter (dust) and minimal energy (cold). Entropy in living things is aging and death. In regards to matter, it is randomity and chaos.

Life or ectropy works to organize matter and energy into ever more complex and powerful systems. Entropy or decay works to disrupt and downgrade energy systems into chaos and death. You can see these forces at work in your organization. Your organization is ectropic; it is striving to organize people, energies, and materials to create desired results. However, within your organization there are also entropic forces that create disorganization and losses of time and energy. As an executive, manager or supervisor; you are always trying to increase ectropy and decrease entropy.

All the physical matter and physical energies in your organization left to themselves, are naturally entropic. The Life force in your organization, the intelligence, creativity, and abilities of your employees, are ectropic and work against the natural entropy of the physical universe. The success of your organization depends on how well ectropy wins over entropy.

The Positive Emotions such as enthusiasm and passion are ectropic. The Negative Emotions such as anger, fear, resentment, and hate are entropic – which is why you need to get them out of your organization. The main problem that you have in this battle between ectropy and entropy in your organization is the entropy that appears within your ectropic force, your people, in the form of their Negative Quantum Energies, particularly their Negative Emotions. The Negative Emotions are painful to people and they do everything in their power to try to stop or change them. They must do so because they obey the Existential Imperative, the ultimate human motivation of all human behavior.

When people are living in the Fatal Paradigm, the belief that events outside of you create your happiness, that they are not the creator of their emotions, and therefore external events are; they must attack externals with Negative Energy to change, stop or destroy them as the apparent cause of their pain. The externals in this case are the organization and the other people in it. That

Negative Energy is entropic, both internally to the person and his happiness, and externally to others and the organization.

Only Life is intelligent. Only Life is causal. Only Life is creative. Life is the only ectropic force in the universe ,although as we have just seen above, it can also be entropic in that it can create Negative Energy and therefore damage and destruction.

BEings are individual Life entities. They are (or can be) agents of ectropy, the only ones that exist. Matter is always entropic; left alone without the attention of ectropic Life entities (BEings, people) it will decay into the homogenous, lowest energy, random, undistinguished, dust.

Therefore to understand BE and BEings, we must understand Life. Above all, we must understand what determines when Life is ectropic (creative) versus entropic (destructive). These are the forces that you must control in yourself and in your organization to make it more ectropic, more alive, more powerful.

What is Life, the ectropic force in the universe? What are the characteristics and qualities of Life? One way to answer this question is to ask yourself what are the differences between a rock and plant and animal and a human being, as each represents a different level of Life. Let's make the question easy by just taking the two ends of the polarity, Matter <> Life, and just asking what are the differences between you and a rock. What are the differences between you, or any person, and a rock?

We can answer with such things as awareness, perception, consciousness, intelligence, knowledge, memory, will, decision, creativity, self-esteem, value, the ability to love, value and the ability to emote and to feel emotions, which is the ability to be happy and to suffer. A rock is not much good at any of that. So the difference between your BEing and the BEing of a rock is notable. The difference between you and the rock is the Life Energies.

Observing that many of these energies are similar or related, let us organize all these characteristics, qualities, and abilities in a table of four columns. The first column groups all those properties related to Consciousness and Knowledge. The second column consists of all the characteristics related to Cause, to Power. The third column contains those related to the estimation or assignation of Value. The fourth column is the Emotional Energy Spectrum that we saw in the previous chapter.

The Life Energy is really one Energy, but it contains these four "rays". Think of white light going through a prism. One light enters, and four colors of the rainbow come out. That is how the Life Energy is one and four at the same time.

The ONE Life Energy Has Four Main Component Energies

Consciousness	Cause	Value	Emotion/ FEEL+/-
Awareness	Will	Assign Relative Value	Positive FEEL
Perception	Word, Promise, Commitment	Good < > Bad	Positive Emotions
Experience	Decision	Assign Value to Self, Self-Esteem	Happiness
Distinction	Change, Move	Assign Value to Others	
Know	Determination	Deserve < > Undeserving	
Intuition	Persistence	Worthy < > Unworthy	
Memory	Design, Plan	Less Than < > More Than	Negative FEEL
Intelligence	Order, Organize	Inferior < > Superior	Negative Emotions
Creativity	CREATE	Should Be < > Should Not Be	UPS: Unhappiness, Pains & Suffering

For each column, one word is assigned that will represent all the forms of energy in that column. The following labels are used: Wisdom, Power, and Value. The last column, we will call Emotions for the moment to remind us that it is the Emotions Energy Polarity and the Happiness <> Pain polarity. Do not forget that these two, Emotions and Happiness are the same Energy. To the average person this will not make any sense because we have been raised to understand that joy is just one of the emotions.

Thus, the summary and the "bottom line" labels for each column are:

WISDOM   POWER   VALUE   EMOTION

Life (aka spirit) consists of these four Energies. A BEing, whether a plant, animal, or human, is a Life entity and so has some degree of these four Life Energies. As you are a BEing, you are made up of the four energies. Notice that these energies are non-physical; they are spiritual: they are the Quantum Energies.

These four energies are the Essence, the Nucleus of what you are as a Life-Energy entity, as a spirit. These are the four Human Nuclear Energies. They are subtle Energies, but at the same time, they are the most powerful of all Energies that exist. They are the most powerful Energies because they are the full object of the Existential Imperative. To BE-FEEL more and more positive of these Energies is the ultimate motivation of all human effort and behavior. The quest to BE and FEEL more Nuclear Energy is what moves all of mankind.

To BE-FEEL the positive polarities of these Energies, and

96

to avoid BE-FEELing the negative polarities of these Human Nuclear Energies, is the ultimate motivation of all human behavior. The Existential Imperative of every individual to control these Energies within is the most powerful force in the world. It is the force that has and continues to shape all personal lives and history itself. Understand and harness it in your life and organization, and watch things take off like a space shuttle. Businesses, teams and groups that are able to recognize and increase the Life Energy of its employees are guaranteed a calmer, logical and productive workforce.

When the first letter of the words, Wisdom, Power, Value, and Emotion are capitalized they are referenced as the Nuclear Energies of BEing.

CHAPTER 7

BEing: Your IDentities At Work

The ultimate motivation of every human being is to BE-FEEL , BE and FEEL, more Life, more Nuclear Energy, more Spirit. The ultimate motivation of every person is to be—or have more—BEing: more Wisdom, more Power, more Value (self-esteem), more Positive Emotion = more Joy/Happiness. This is the Existential Imperative: more Life = more BEing = more Wisdom, Power, Value.

Each of the Nuclear Energies is a polarity; each has a positive and negative side. You will remember from our chapter on Polarity that negative must exist for the positive to exist. You create which of the first three Nuclear Energies you BE (are), and which polarity of that energy you BE (are) by means of your IDentities.[13]

---

13 IDentity spelled with the first two letters capitalizes distinguish these words as Quantum Energies. An identity can include such things such as social roles—I am a parent, for example. "Identity" in this book refers to the Nuclear Energy IDentities of Life.

IDentities

An identity is any creation of self. An Identity is any declaration you make about what or who you are; or what or who you are not. Most identities take the form of "I am", or "I am not".[14] As you are the absolute creator of all your Quantum Energies, your declaration of **What You Are** or **What You Are Not** is all that is necessary to make it so.

The following table will make the Nuclear IDentities Polarities clear. Under each of the three Nuclear Energies, there are listed several forms of expression for that IDentity. These are only examples; there are many other ways to express that identity. The phrasing used to express an IDentity is unimportant. It is the concept of declaring or denying you are that polarity of that Nuclear Energy that is important. The exact words used to state that declaration are irrelevant.

Examples of the Nuclear Energy IDentities that determine BEing, What or Who you are BEing at any moment, in relation to any other person or event.

Positive Nuclear IDentities

WISDOM	POWER	VALUE
I Am Intelligent	I Am Capable	I Am Worthy
I Am Creative	I Can Do It	I Deserve

14 A few identities are verbs, such as I can<> I can't; and I deserve <> I don't deserve.

I Know	I Am Strong	I Am Good Enough
I Am Smart	I Am A Success	I Am Important
I Learn Easily	I Am Powerful	I Am Valuable

Negative Nuclear IDentities

ANTI-WISDOM	ANTI-POWER	ANTI-VALUE
I Am Ignorant	I Can't; I Am Unable	I Am Not Worthy
I Am Dumb	I Am Incapable	I Don't Deserve
I Am Stupid	I Am Weak	I Am Less Than Others
I Can't Learn	I Am Useless	I Am Not Good Enough
Studying is Hard	I Am a Failure	Nobody Loves Me

The Existential Imperative, the ultimate motivation, is to BE-FEEL the Positive Nuclear Identities as much as possible (which obviously implies to avoid or get out of the negative polarities.)

A review of important concepts thus far:

1) Emotional energy is a polarity. In order for the positive experience of anything to exist, the negative experience must also exist.

2) The emotional energy polarity, and the Happiness <>UPS (Unhappiness, Pain & Suffering) polarity are the same energy, the same polarity. Your happiness or pain in life is purely emotional.

3) External events are never the cause of the Emotion = Happiness <> Pain Polarity – You are now about to see what is.

The Fourth Nuclear Energy, Emotions:

It is important to note how your experience of Positive <> Negative Emotion impacts your actions. Consider what the emotions DO. They are energy in motion, e-motion, e-motive, e-motivation. Motivation is what moves people. Emotional energy is what motivates and moves the human being, both positively and negatively. Observe what each polarity of your Emotional Energy motivates, what DO's (actions and behaviors) do they encourage? Do not the Positive Emotions: contentment, satisfaction, affection, delight, enthusiasm, passion, love and joy energize people to approach, unite, integrate, encourage, construct, support, care for, improve, increase and grow things (be those things your children, your plants, your pets, or your organization)?

Now look at what the Negative Emotions DO: (anger, resentment, hate, guilt, fear, sorrow, grief, depression) Do they not energize people to behave just the opposite: to avoid, flee from, attack, punish, separate, divorce, harm, damage, or destroy?

Now consider again FEELing. FEELing is an emotion. FEELing is Happiness +/-. Emotion +/- and Happiness+/- are the same energy. Your Positive and Negative Emotions are simply different modulations and degrees of Happiness +/-.

Take a closer look at the FEEL of the Negative Emotions: When you feel anger are you happy? When you feel fear are you happy? If you feel grief, are you happy? You need no one to tell you what happiness is: you FEEL it and you know it. You FEEL it inside of you, and you know it when other people dump on you (their anger, invalidation, blame, manipulation, lies, resentment, hate, etc.) Your Negative and Positive Emotions determine your experience of happiness or pain.

Internally, your experience of Happiness +/- is how you FEEL, which can be anywhere along the Emotions Polarity Spectrum.

Externally, physically, your Happiness +/- is your actions (DO) towards others. Positive Emotion is any kind of energy that motivates, encourages, aids, supports, heals, builds, grows, integrates or unites things or people, or an Energy System (such as your family or organization).

Negative Emotional Energy is any kind of energy that discourages, retards, avoids, separates, divorces, harms, damages, or destroys things or people.

Thus, Happiness <> Pain is both how you FEEL internally (the Emotional Energy Spectrum), and the actions (DO) that you take externally towards others, which either aid or harm.

You can see the Causal Sequence at work here: FEEL→DO; FEELing motivates DOing (Action). Our FEELings of Happiness <> Pain prompt the rest of the Causal Sequence. Life works FEEL → THINK → DO → HAVE (ignoring the BE for the moment).

You are a spirit, a spiritual[15] BEing. You are made of the Life

---

15 Do not confuse spirit and spiritual with religious. They are very different concepts. Spirit is simply a non-physical Life Energy entity. You are a spirit whether you may or may not subscribe to one of the thousands of religions and sects on the planet.

Energy that expresses in the Four Nuclear Energies, of which one is <u>Emotions = Happiness +/-</u>. You know it when you FEEL it and when you see it. Emotion+/- (along with the other three Nuclear Energies that together make up Life or Spirit) is the most powerful energy on the planet. Every human being is seeking it, because it is Life Energy itself.

What grows your organization is Positive Emotional Energy.

What harms your organization is Negative Emotional Energy. What motivates people to perform well and contribute their best is their experience of Positive Energy. What motivates people to resistance, conflicts, and sabotage is Negative Energy. What grows your organization is the Positive Energy of enthusiasm, passion, interest, commitment, determination, initiative, resourcefulness of your people. What most harms your organization is the Negative Quantum Energy of anger, fear, resentment, hate, indifference, apathy, etc. Until a person understands the Fourth Nuclear Energy, Emotion +/-; they will not be able to control this energy, in themselves or in their groups and organizations. So what causes and controls this Energy?

The answer lies in the Causal Sequence:

BE → FEEL → THINK → DO → HAVE

Your BEing determines your experience of Positive or Negative Emotion. It works like this:

Your BEing is composed of the four Nuclear Energies. The polarity of the first three, Wisdom, Power, and/or Value, is what determines the polarity of the fourth Energy, Emotions. The polarity and strength of the fourth Energy, Happiness, depends on the polarity and strength of any or all of the first three, Wisdom – Power - Value (WPV). Thus, your Emotional Energy, which we denominate FEEL in the Causal Sequence, is actually the Fourth of the four Nuclear Energies of BEing. FEEL is the last part of BE. BE-FEEL are so related that you cannot separate them. Here is one of the greatest laws for your personal and organizational success:

Your Emotions are your Positive or Negative Emotion for yourself, according to the Nuclear IDentity you are adopting in relation to an event.

- When you are in a Positive Nuclear IDentity (Wisdom, Power, or Value) you will naturally feel Positive Energy and celebrate yourself. You will experience that Positive Energy as the Positive Emotions: joy, happiness, enthusiasm, interest, passion, satisfaction, high self esteem and love.

- When you are in a Negative Nuclear IDentity, denying Wisdom or Knowing (Anti-Wisdom); denying Power (Anti-Power); or denying Value (Anti-Value) you will be in Negative Energy. You will experience that Negative Energy as Negative Emotions such as anger, sadness, guilt, resentment, hate, anxiety, fear or depression.

This is illustrated in the following diagram:

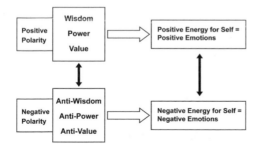

105

To rephrase this most important Law:

Your only happiness or pain in life is your own Positive or Negative Emotional Energy about your Self where that Self is determined by the Nuclear IDentity that you are adopting in relation to the events of your life.

In other words, your emotions are showing you–and everybody around you—who you are BEing.

If you are in Positive Emotions, you are BE-FEELing your Self as Wise, Powerful, or Valuable. If you are in Negative Emotions, you are BE-FEELing yourself as foolish, stupid, unable, weak, unworthy, or not good enough.

A simple example will illustrate all of this. Imagine that there is a large snake crawling across the floor in a crowded room. How will people react? Some will go into Negative Emotions such as fear, panic, loathing, and want to run away. Others may want to attack the snake to kill it. These are Negative Energy reactions. Others will calmly move themselves out of the way, a neutral or SPace reaction.

You have undoubtedly seen programs on the Discovery, National Geographic, or Animal Planet television channels where some people go out into the wild and actually look for snakes, including the most dangerous ones. When they find one, they run up to it, pick it up, hold it carefully and lovingly, even caress it. Some of them almost kiss them. These are Positive Energy reactions.

First of all, note that once again we have the same external event and varying human emotions and reactions that run the entire Polarity Spectrum from most negative to most positive.

Once again we see that external events do not cause human emotional experience.

However, what we are most interested in here is what determines their emotions– and that is the Nuclear IDentities they are activating in relation to the event, the snake crawling across the floor in a crowded room. The people who are activating Negative Emotions are doing so because they are activating Negative Nuclear IDentities (NIRs[16]). In relation to the snake, they are activating identities of **I don't know** enough about snakes (Anti-Wisdom); **I can't control** the snake; **it is more powerful than I; it can harm me** and **I won't be able to prevent it**. Notice how these are Anti-Power IDentities (The first is an Anti-Wisdom ID). These people are in Negative Emotional Energy to self and therefore to the snake. Ignorant of their internal mechanisms of BE-FEEL, they think the snake causes their pain, but it is not the snake, it is their IDentity in relation to the snake that they are emoting about.

It appears that the snake is the cause of their Negative Emotions = Pain. This is an illusion. The real cause is their generation of Negative Energy for self in the NIRs (Negative IDentities) that they are assuming in relation to the snake. Not understanding this creates the illusion that external events cause your Negative Emotions and so make you unhappy. That illusion then sends people on the impossible dream and quest of trying to control external events (i.e. others) to control their emotions and

---

16 NIR is the abbreviation for Negative IDentity Realities, which is another term for Negative Nuclear IDentities. PIR is the abbreviation for Positive IDentity Realities, which is another way to say Positive Nuclear IDentities. Identities appears with the first two letters capitalized to show that these are Quantum Energies.

be happy. Worse yet, they then use Negative Energy to try to control others with anger, blame, invalidation, punishment or sabotage.

At the other end of the spectrum, we have those people who have a Positive Energy reaction to the snake, those that approach it and care for it. These people are in Positive Emotions—interest and enthusiasm. As we have seen these are self-love emotions. These people are activating Positive Nuclear IDentities (PIRs) such as **I know** about snakes (Wisdom). **I can handle** this snake; **I am more powerful** than the snake; **I am able** to prevent it from harming me (Power). Their Positive Emotions, apparently for the snake and their ability to handle the situation, are the activation and projection of their Positive Energy for themselves in these Positive Nuclear IDentities.

Again it appears that the snake is the cause of their emotions, their happiness, but not so; it is their PIRs, their Positive IDentities, their self-love in the form of their Positive Emotions.

In another example, your boss has a meeting and announces that the company is not meeting profit objectives therefore everyone's personal sales objective has been raised to $20,000 per month. Those in Positive IDentity will embrace the opportunity; those in Negative IDentity (I can't do it) will panic.

Not understanding the cause of emotions creates the illusion that external events cause your Positive Emotions and so make you happy. This sends you chasing a mirage of happiness in the external world. "If only I can finally find that right thing that causes happiness and accumulate enough of it, one day I will finally and permanently be happy." (It ain't happening so don't hold your breath.)

Very important: Make sure you see here how the illusion that external events cause pain and can make us happy develops. Be sure that you understand that it is not the events, but the identities you assume that generate the Emotion +/- = Happiness +/- Polarity Energy. Any person who does not understand this will never be able to increase their level of happiness in life. They will be chasing external mirages instead of controlling the real, internal cause.

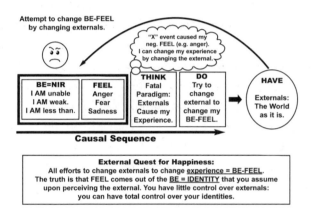

Your Point of Power for Happiness:

1) You cannot and never will control most events in your life. You cannot control what other people say and do; nor the big events of life such as accidents, illnesses, loss of job, loss of money.

2) You cannot directly control your emotions. They are automatic energy responses to Who You Are, to the Life, to the Spirit in you, as defined by your Nuclear IDentities. Negation, suppression and substance abuse do not count as control and are unhealthy.

3) Your Point of Power in Life is that you can control Who You Are, your Nuclear IDentities.

In the determination of Who You Are, in creation of your Self, you are Emperor. Your word is law.

You can eliminate the Negative IDentities, and create and energize the positive ones to make them your permanent experience. You can make your creation of Self impervious to external events. You can learn to hold your position of BEing Positive Nuclear IDentities. You can stop letting Who You Are be controlled and determined by external things. This is the only workable way to Happiness, because the only happiness that exists is the Positive Emotion you automatically generate when you are BEing Love-able, when you are BEing Wisdom, Power, and Value. You have here the Essence of Life. The ultimate motivation of all human beings is to be more Life, to BE-FEEL more of the four Nuclear Energies of Wisdom, Power, Value, leading to your experience of Positive Energy.

You now understand the Causal Sequence:

BE → FEEL[17] → THINK → DO → HAVE, and how BE causes FEEL.

You can now understand that all THINK DO HAVE has as its purpose to make the person BE somebody so that they FEEL good. Going outside of yourself to try to control the world to control your BE-FEEL, your happiness, is called the **External Quest**.

The External Quest to control BE-FEEL (IDentities and Emotions = Happiness) by trying to use external things (success,

---

17 Because FEEL cannot be separated from BE, it is often written as a hyphenated word.

fame, power, money, relationships, suppression with drugs, tobacco, alcohol, etc.) to reach happiness is impossible. THINK → DO → HAVE does not control BE-FEEL. You can move your FEEL, spike it momentarily with a MOP (Moment of Pleasure), but no amount of DOing and HAVEing will ever make a permanent change in your BEing and therefore in your FEELing = Happiness. Getting something in the external world may trigger a MOP, but these are always fleeting. No amount of Doing and having will ever make a permanent change in your BEing and therefore in your FEELing = Happiness.

To make permanent changes in your BE-FEEL, in the Spirit Life Energy that you are; to live continually expanding your Nuclear Energy, the amount of Wisdom, Power, Value, and Positive Emotion that you are and experience; you must learn how to work directly with these energies. You must learn how to discreate your Negative Nuclear IDentities and to create and strengthen your Positive IDentities.

To stop the generation of Negative Energy in your organization, your employees must also understand these things. Everyone must understand that external events and other people do not cause their emotions; that they themselves create their own emotional experience. They must understand that what does cause their emotions is their Nuclear IDentities. As long as they don't understand these two things, their lives will continue as they are now, and your organization will continue to operate in Negative Quantum Energy.

When a person or an organization transforms itself from resisting and fighting against others to control their own internal Negative Nuclear IDentities and starts supporting each other in creating and operating in the Positive Nuclear IDentities; the entire energy climate and system transforms. A whole new level of power and job satisfaction—joy on the job—awakens.

CHAPTER 8

Activations and Discreation

A n event that activates a Negative IDentity and its charge of Negative Emotion, is called a "trigger event" or just "trigger". In the previous chapter, we used the example of a snake. The snake appears, and the person unconsciously adopts, assumes, activates, or triggers a Negative IDentity. The snake is the trigger, but not the cause of the Negative Emotion.

The trigger is not the cause of the Negative IDentity and its accompanying painful self-directed Negative Emotional charge. The Negative IDentity and its emotional pain already exist as an energy mass in the subconscious of the person. Every human being has hundreds of these Negative IDentity masses. Think of them as a recording of "who we were", made usually in our childhood when we did not have much Wisdom, Power, or Value compared to the adults around us. And of course, many adults reinforce such ideas of ignorant, stupid, weak or valueless self on children by their treatment and invalidation of them. (Thus, you can see the importance of preserving the self-esteem of children.)

We call the triggering and movement of a Negative Nuclear IDentity with its Negative Emotion charge from the subconscious to the consciousness (experience) of a person an "activation". We call the Nuclear IDentity plus the emotional charge a mass of energy, an IDentity mass. An activation is the triggering and movement of a Negative IDentity mass (IDentity plus Emotion) from the subconscious to the perception and FEELing of the person.

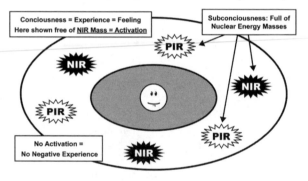

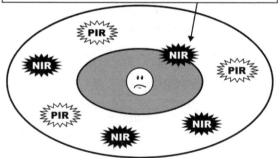

There are many ways that Nuclear IDentity Mass activations can affect us. The most obvious is simply the FEELing of any Negative Emotion. However, many people have their emotions blocked to one degree or another. In such cases, activations can be experienced as the sudden oncoming of heaviness, tiredness, a desire to nap, wanting to get away, headache or pressures in the head, and as sensations and pains in the body. It is common that an activated person does not perceive the Negative Nuclear IDentities, but they are always present. They can be obscured either by the sheer amount of the emotional charge, or by the person's blocks to his negative experience. People who are accustomed to handling life by thinking often have their feeling blocked.

The Causal Sequence, remember, is:

BE-FEEL → THINK → DO → HAVE

Put the trigger in front of that and you have:

Trigger → BE-FEEL → THINK → DO → HAVE

Here is how this reads:

A trigger event occurs. The person unconsciously activates (adopts) a Negative Nuclear IDentity, which is automatically accompanied by a Negative Emotional Energy charge. A Negative Energy such as anger or fear, creates turbulence in his mind (THINK) as he automatically, consciously or subconsciously, starts computing what to DO to stop, change, punish, destroy, or get something (HAVE) (or use some chemical to suppress) that will counter attack that trigger and so change his experience. Remember that in the Fatal Paradigm, I am not Cause, therefore something outside of me must be, s/he sees the trigger as the cause of their pain, and will use their anger, resentment, or hate to attack the trigger.

This is the basic mechanism of all negative human behavior, especially of all relationship conflicts and problems. It is mostly subconscious and entirely automatic. Until people understand the mechanism, there is little hope to control or change it.

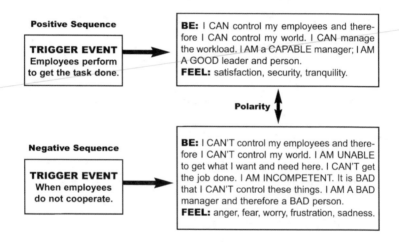

Positive Sequence

TRIGGER EVENT
Employees perform
to get the task done.

BE: I CAN control my employees and therefore I CAN control my world. I CAN manage the workload. I AM a CAPABLE manager; I AM A GOOD leader and person.
FEEL: satisfaction, security, tranquility.

Polarity

Negative Sequence

TRIGGER EVENT
When employees
do not cooperate.

BE: I CAN'T control my employees and therefore I CAN'T control my world. I AM UNABLE to get what I want and need here. I CAN'T get the job done. I AM INCOMPETENT. It is BAD that I CAN'T control these things. I AM A BAD manager and therefore a BAD person.
FEEL: anger, fear, worry, frustration, sadness.

NOT BAD or WRONG:

It is important to understand that Negative Nuclear Identities, Negative Emotions, and activations are not bad and they are not wrong. They are an essential part of human existence as by the Laws of Polarity, they must exist for a person to be able to experience their opposites: Wisdom, Power, Value and Positive Emotions. Thus, they are human. Every person has them without exception. Furthermore, they transcend language, culture, economic class and nationality. Every person, without exception, has the same NIRs. They differ in combinations and intensities and what it takes to activate them. Of course, many people do all kinds of psychological somersaults to suppress, hide or disguise that they have them. Ego is used by many managers as an attempt to compensate for the lack of Positive Wisdom, Power and Value. When a person is operating from Ego, they will seek to tear down others in order to elevate self—which is to compensate NIRs.

The problem is not that you and others have Negative Nuclear Identities, but that you do not take responsibility for them and your activations. Problems arise as people go through life blaming their pain on others and then dumping Negative Energy on them to punish or stop them as their triggers.

DISCREATION

You can control, to a certain extent, your activations just by understanding what is happening, taking responsibility for your Negative Emotions, and ceasing to dump your Negative Energy on others. However, the optimum solution is always to discreate the Negative IDentity masses. This permanently eliminates the Negative Nuclear IDentity and its Negative Emotional charge from your subconscious. The general principles are:

- Experience experienced discharges and discreates.
- Resistance causes Persistence.

You discreate your Negative Nuclear IDentities simply by

allowing yourself to BE-FEEL that way until they discreate; you have only to experience them fully. You currently refuse to experience your Negative IDentities because you believe them as bad to BE that way. You resist BE-FEELing anything bad. Thus, we have the sequence Bad → Resistance. Resistance causes pain and persistence. Your Negative IDentities are not good or bad; they are just one side of the Nuclear Energy Polarity. They must exist – but you don't have to BE them.

As Resistance Causes Persistence, you must first discreate this resistance to BE-FEEL your NIRs, your Negative IDentities, by experiencing your resistance until it discreates. Once you no longer resist BEing that way, which is, after all, your own creation of self, you will then allow yourself to experience that IDentity fully, letting yourself BE and FEEL that way. This will eventually discreate it.

EXAMPLES

Example 1: In preparing the quarterly statements for your team, you inadvertently carry last year's figures on the spreadsheet. You neglect to proof-read the document and the incorrect information is circulated throughout the company. It reaches the vice-president before the error is found.

You activate FEELing embarrassment and sadness. You feel underneath that and find Anti-Wisdom: I AM Stupid. Your mind (THINK) goes wild: "How could I have made such a stupid error? Now everyone in the company knows that I am an idiot."

What can you do? It has happened. There is no point in continuing to resist the incident with additional Negative Energy.

To do so is actually counter-productive as like-energy attracts like energy. To discreate your Negative Nuclear IDentity in this example:

1. Discreate your resistance to I AM AN IDIOT by experiencing how bad it is to be an idiot and how much you do not want to be an idiot.
2. Open your FEELing and let yourself BE-FEEL an idiot. What does this flavor of energy called "idiot", this creation of self, FEEL like? Simply experience it until it discreates.

You will feel Negative Emotions such as discomfort, pain, anger, sadness, regret, fear, but it will discreate and you will be restored to serenity.

Example 2: You have been a manager in charge of the housekeeping department for 10 years. In a merger of departments, housekeeping will be combined with maintenance. Your position is down-graded to supervisor.

You activate in anger, then grief, sadness, and finally apathy. You FEEL beneath the emotion and find Anti-Value IDentities are activated: I AM UNIMPORTANT. I DON'T MATTER. NOBODY APPRECIATES ME.

1. Discreate your resistance to BEing of low value (worth, importance) by experiencing out how bad it is to be worthless and tossed to the side (or whatever comes up for you); and how much you do not want to BE worthless.

2. Open your FEELing and let yourself BE unimport-
    ant, unwanted. What does this energy, this creation
    FEEL like? Experience it until it discreates.

Example 3: You are interested in transferring to another department. The new job requires that you climb utility poles and
lift heavy equipment up to 75 pounds. You take the exam three
times and fail. You are permanently disqualified.

Your emotional experience: frustration, anger and disap-
pointment. You explore your experience underneath the emotions and find Anti-Power IDentities. I COULDN'T DO IT, I
AM UNABLE; I AM WEAK; I AM A FAILURE.

1. Discreate your resistance to BEing each of the forms
    of Anti-Power by experiencing out how bad it is to
    be unable and a failure; and how much you do not
    want to BE so incapable and weak.
2. Open your FEELing and let yourself BE unable and
    a failure, etc. What does this energy, this creation
    FEEL like? Experience it until it discreates.

In the above examples, you may think that allowing yourself
to BE-FEEL these Negative IDentities would affirm them. Just
the opposite. Resistance to BEing them makes them Persist. It is
the BEing and FEELing of them that lets the energy discharge
from them, much like letting the air out of balloon. The difference is: Will and mind create. Experience discreates. Be sure not
to confuse thinking about something with FEELing. They are
two entirely different things.

In order to create a life of joy and serenity you must begin to confront your negative experiences. There are many personal growth systems available to you however most will place an emphasis on creating the positive experiences you seek using techniques such as affirmations and visualization–which is creation, not discreation. If you have used these techniques in the past then you know they are usually abandoned after a few days. The reason for this is that under your positive intention lies your negative BE. Often an affirmation that is contrary to your current (negative) BE will trigger that IDentity.

Any serious attempts to create a positive change will activate negatives. Sooner or later you will have to confront your negative experiences if your desire is to be a person of more Wisdom, Power and Value. Do not plaster over your negative BE-FEEL with positives. This does not repair the underlying structure. Discreate the negative, and then the positive will shine forth at the lightest touch of your creation Energy. On your growth journey you will begin to see your negative experiences for what they truly are–opportunities to create a more powerful, loving and wiser you.

CHAPTER 9

Cause <> Effect

T here are three fundamental forces in life that a person must understand to control his life, be powerful, and achieve success, love, happiness, and joy. The three are Cause, SPace, and Energy. All three are introduced in this book, beginning with the Cause<>Effect Polarity Spectrum.

To change the energy climate of your organization, you must move your people up the Cause <> Effect Polarity Spectrum from Victim to Response-ability.

Definitions: Cause

The Positive Pole of the Cause <> Effect Polarity

Noun: The agent of force and action that effects change. That which originates, initiates, creates, manifests, decides, determines, acts, forms, produces, gives, moves, controls, changes, or affects anything. The positive pole of the Cause<>Effect Polarity. The concept of Cause includes: Will, Power, Force, Creator, Creation, and Production.

Verb: The action and process of bringing into being or changing something. The action of originating, starting, creating, controlling, changing, moving, producing, affecting, or effecting something. The action of producing an Effect.

Cause is Power; it is the ability to produce the desired results; it is your ability to manifest what you want in life.

Definitions: Effect

The Negative Pole of the Cause <> Effect Polarity.

Noun: The influence, change, affect or result produced by a Cause. Examples: The effect of a bomb is destruction. The effect of a Quantum reality on consciousness is experience. Synonyms: result, impact, outcome.

Verb: To cause something, to create an effect, to produce an effect, to carry out an action to a successful result.

The condition of Effect in people is a condition of no power, no control; of being affected or controlled by an external cause. This is also known as the condition of Victim.

So far you have seen that you are Cause; that you and every human being is the sole Creator of his Quantum experience, which includes identities, thoughts, and emotions. You have lived to this point in Victim of the world in regards to your emotions. If you have understood everything to this point, you are making a transition to knowing that you are Response-able for your emotions. You are no longer the Victim of events, you are moving to Cause. It is only from this understanding, this stand in life, that you have POWER to control your emotions that are the only Happiness <> Suffering in life.

As shown, the basic problem of Negative Energy in life, whether inside you, in your family, or in your organization, is that most people think they are Effect. They believe that external events cause their emotions, their suffering. They also think that externals (including the organization) should and could cause their happiness—if only they could get them to behave "right". This belief of "I am Not-Cause; therefore I am at the Effect of Externals" is the Fatal IDentity and the Fatal Paradigm. Together they create the condition of Victim.

You will recall that an identity is a declaration of self. In this case, the Fatal IDentity is the IDentity I am not Cause; I am not Creator. On Creating this IDentity, the person does not stop himself from being creator, but he does blind himself to the perception of being creator. In other words, he shoots himself in the foot.

The Fatal Paradigm is the natural result and the other side of the Fatal IDentity. "Given that I am not Cause-Creator, then externals things must be." Thus, the person assigns Cause to external events, which automatically places him in the position of Effect. The condition of Effect is the condition of Victim.

The Fatal IDentity → Fatal Paradigm starts with the Anti-Power IDentity that "I am Effect and Powerless; that externals cause my experience, my suffering. As I have little power over externals, I am their helpless and hapless Victim. I am powerless; externals have the power over my life."

This automatically activates the Negative Emotions of frustration, anger, rage, resentment, desperation, hate, helplessness, impotence, sadness, and depression. Furthermore, the person can see no way out, because (from his perspective) he has no Power in the situation. Externals have all the power.

Happiness is impossible when a person is in the Fatal IDentity-Paradigm. What you will get from the people in this mode of operation in life is lots of low morale, irresponsibility, laziness, Negative Energy, conflicts, and problems. Is any of this happening in your business? Now get up close and personal— is any of this happening in your life?

To "fix" the Quantum Energy System of a person which is essential to "fix" the Group Energy System of a relationship, a family, or an organization, you must start by "fixing" where the person is operating on the Cause-Effect Polarity Spectrum, and show him a way out of his Nuclear Anti-Power IDentities about life. You take a person out of Victim by showing him that he does have control, that he is response-able. Response-ability is the midpoint, the transition point between Cause-Power and Effect-Victim, as shown in the following diagram:

Comparison of Characteristics of Cause and of Effect in people:

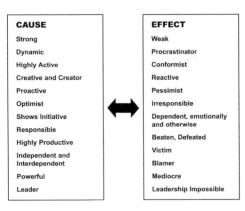

CAUSE	EFFECT
Strong	Weak
Dynamic	Procrastinator
Highly Active	Conformist
Creative and Creator	Reactive
Proactive	Pessimist
Optimist	Irresponsible
Shows Initiative	Dependent, emotionally and otherwise
Responsible	Beaten, Defeated
Highly Productive	Victim
Independent and Interdependent	Blamer
Powerful	Mediocre
Leader	Leadership Impossible

Definitions:

Proactive: A person who is ahead of events; who foresees consequences and events and takes action in time to prevent or control the negative ones and to produce the positive ones. Such a person is at Cause.

Reactive: A person who is behind events; who fails to see things coming or fails to take action in time to prevent or control the negative ones. A person who is emotionally reactive to others and events; who activates easily with the Negative Emotions such as anger, resentment, guilt, fear, sorrow.

The Polarity Scale of CAUSE <> EFFECT

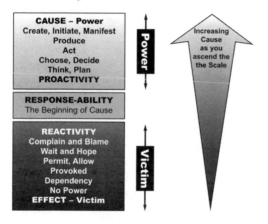

Every human being is operating at some point on the Cause-Effect Polarity Scale above. Furthermore, your level changes from situation to situation. For example, you may be Cause and Creative in your work world, but a Victim in your relationships.

The above table summarizes the characteristics of Cause versus those of Effect in people.

CHAPTER 10

Response-ability

> *Responsibility is a unique concept. It can only reside in a single individual. You may share it with others, but your portion is not diminished. You may delegate it, but it is still with you. You may disclaim it, but you cannot divest yourself of it.*
>
> *—Admiral Hyman Rickover*

To transform the energy climate and improve the profitability of your organization, you must move people from Victim to Response-ability[18]. The condition of Effect-Victim ends, and the state of Cause-Power starts with the Declaration of Response-ability. Responsability is a make or break point in life, the point of transformation between:

---

18 Note that "responsability" is spelled with an "a" to indicate that we are going far beyond the normal idea of responsibility, and including all the concepts and definitions of this chapter.

Effect = Victim and Cause = Power.

If you are already in a condition of Responsability for your life and everything in it, congratulations. However, most people are not in a condition of Responsability. The Denial of Responsability creates the condition of Victim. Living in a condition of No-Responsability = Victim guarantees a life of:

- Low Personal Power (not getting much of what you want in life).
- Frequent Anti-Power IDentity activations (I can't get it; I can't control it)
- Poor self-image, low self-esteem (low power, loser, failure)
- Negative Emotions, unhappiness and suffering. (frustration, sadness, depression)
- Complaining and blaming (others for one's problems).
- Relationship problems and conflicts (the other is always at fault and should change– but won't)
- In organizations: low degree of: responsability, initiative, creativity, resourcefulness, and production. High degrees of errors and omission, poor customer service, problems and conflicts of all kinds.

It is, in fact, impossible to be happy in a condition of Denial of Responsability =Victim.

The Concept of Responsability:

- Responsability = Response + Ability.
- Response-ability is the ability to respond.

- To respond to or for something is to take action (DO) in some way to handle that thing or situation.
- Responsability, then, is the ability to act. To act is to be in a condition of CAUSE (defined in the previous chapter).
- Responsable, Responsability = Able To Act.

Some of the Definitions of Responsability:

1. Any condition of possibility of action, including when experiencing negative effects caused by others. If you can act to avoid or remedy something, you are response-able.
2. Consciousness of Cause; acknowledgement and awareness of being Cause, of being able to act. To say, "I am Responsable", is to say, "I am Cause" in the matter.
3. The ability to respond deliberately under self-control and reason; as opposed to out-of-control emotional reaction. Logical choice and control, as opposed to emotional reactivity and resistance.
4. The ability to vary your actions and responses until you achieve the desired result (as opposed to repeating over and over an ingrained habit or behavioral rut).
5. The duty or privilege to care for someone or something, which is to be at Cause for its well-being. (Such as Parent-Child)
6. Accountability (Justice): The ability and the duty

to respond for our negative actions, to restore damaged or lost energy. Without Accountability, Responsability does not exist – nor does Justice.

7. The point of change between Effect and Cause on the Cause-Effect Spectrum.

Explanation of each definition:

1. **Responsability is any condition of possibility of action**, especially when at the effect of the negative actions of others (vulnerable to others). In any situation, if you have any possibility of action, then you are responsable—you do not need to be the initial Cause of the situation. For example: you are not responsable for it raining. However, you are responsable for standing outside in it and getting wet as long as you have any possibility of action such as going inside or opening an umbrella. If you have no possibility of action—for example, you are chained to a post—then you have no responsability for getting wet. Any possibility of action establishes responsability. (And if you are chained to the fence, who is responsable for you being chained to the fence –did you do anything that led to getting chained to the fence?)

Here is the key question to determine if you are responseable in any situation where you are suffering negative effects: Do I have any possibility of any kind of action to stop, change or avoid those effects? As an adult, you almost always have some possibility of action in any situation. (Note how it matters not who or what is causing those effects.)

Situation: The company is behind in production and could miss critical customer due dates. The company decides on mandatory overtime for 6 hours for every employee this coming weekend. You have already made plans:

Victim: You tell the wife all plans are cancelled as the company is forcing you to work this weekend. The managers at the company don't know what they are doing and messed up production. You have no choice in the matter.

Creator: You evaluate all options to determine possibility of action. You recall that the union contract allows the company to impose mandatory overtime for a maximum of 6 hours per week. Many employees like overtime and you would probably have no problem finding someone to work your 6 hours plus their own. Worse case, you could always quit and find another job– it is your decision everyday to report to work: you are Cause. After evaluating options you decide the extra money will help. You re-negotiate with your wife to go away next weekend to a higher priced destination or to add in more luxuries on your trip.

2. **Responsability is Consciousness of Cause.** To be responsable is to be aware of Cause, of the duty to act when necessary. When a person declares or believes s/he is not responsable, s/he is declaring s/he need not act; that s/he is not Cause. Responsability, then, is recognition and acceptance of Cause.

Note: As Cause includes decision, initiative, pro-activity and creativity; Denial of Responsability (DOR) impairs all of these.

Situation: Due to a shortfall in profits all departmental budgets are frozen at last year's level. Projected budget needs call for a 15% increase in order to meet production requirements:

Victim: I will not meet annual production quotas. I have done all I can. It is not my fault that the budgets were cut. I am not responsable. The company has tied my hands in this matter.

Creator: I will have to take a closer look at expenditures and determine which will be eliminated. I will look into other vendors that can offer more competitive options. I will investigate establishing a 5 day work week that includes weekends so that overtime can be eliminated.

3.   **The concept of Responsability includes the ability to respond to others and events with self-control and logic**—as opposed to out-of-control Negative Emotional or irrational reaction. It is the ability to respond from reasoned decision in awareness of actions and consequences (Wisdom) as opposed to "knee-jerk" emotional reaction in resistance and effect (reactivity). A person who is response-able acts as opposed to reacts. A person who is at the effect of his Negative Emotions (activated) is reactive rather than response-able—although he is responsable for those reactions nevertheless. When a person is activated, he reacts without thinking and usually with unwise, negative consequences for himself and others.

Situation: You have just heard the news that a promotion has been given to one of your co-workers. You had also applied for the position. You have worked in this department for 15 years and she has worked here for 2 years. You have an exemplary attendance record and have always met your objectives.

Victim: I have had it. This place is unfair. They gave the job to her because they wanted a woman in that position. You storm into your boss's office and demand an explanation. Because of your behavior it is highly unlikely that you will be considered for future opportunities.

Creator: You acknowledge your Negative Energy (frustration, sadness, anger) your Negative Quantum Energy and allow yourself to BE-FEEL your experience of "I AM Powerless" or "I AM Undeserving" and work through it. In doing so, you discreate your Negative Anti-Power or Anti-Value IDentity. You acknowledge that you are interested in moving forward with this company and that you are determined to do so. You ask your boss for a meeting to discuss a developmental plan to enhance your supervisory and technical skills so that you will be prepared for the next promotional opportunity in this and other departments in the company.

4. **The concept of Responsability includes the capacity to vary your actions and responses until you achieve the desired result.** The opposite of this is to repeat over and over any pattern of behavior (communication or action) despite the fact that it does not produce the desired result. A person who is response-able, on not achieving the desired result, will try again using a new approach. A person who is not response-able will keep trying with the same futile approach over and over again, sometimes for years.

In psychology, there is a famous story about this "vary-your-response-ability". In this story, psychologists test rats by hiding cheese in a specific spot in a maze. At the same time, they test humans (using students) by hiding money in a specific spot using as a maze a school laboratory. Both rats and students find the prize (cheese or money) with about equal ability, and both quickly learn to go directly to the hiding spot.

The differences occur when the prize is moved to a new spot. The rats quickly learn that the cheese is no longer in the old spot and respond by concentrating on finding the new spot. They say that the students are still breaking into the laboratory at night looking for the money.

Situation: A hotel has been in business for 60 years. Many of the employees have worked here for numerous years and have become complacent. Profits have steadily declined over the past 10 years as there has been minimal upgrading of office equipment. Scheduling and accounting functions are still being handled manually and the customer base is eroding as customers look for facilities that will meet their technical needs.

Victim: I don't want to learn another process. We've always done it that way in the past and it's worked.

Creator: The world has changed. Our rooms need internet and wireless access. We need voicemail services, automated attendant services and newly decorated guestrooms in order to compete. We can save time and money and streamline our collection processes by mechanizing scheduling and portfolio preparations.

5. Responsability can be the position of caring for

someone or something, or of DOing = Causing something positive. This is a very common usage of the word. Examples: He is responsable for production in the factory. He is responsable for getting the reports out on time.

Situation: You are responsible for preparing the monthly production reports that are reported to the Vice-President. You will be leaving shortly for a 2 week vacation:

Victim: She'll just have to wait. I'll get the information together when I get back.

Creator: Susan is looking for a promotion. I will train her to do the reports in my absence. This will get her the exposure she needs to show that she is a competent employee, the production results will be issued on time and I will have one less thing to handle when I return from vacation.

6. **Accountability: Responsability is the ability and the duty to respond for our actions, including the restoration of any damage we Cause.** This aspect of Responsability is also called Accountability. Accountability is justice; it is the equalization of energy.

There are two sides to accountability. The first is the positive side: that positive results be rewarded. The second side is the negative side. S/He who produces negative results is responsable (is to be at Cause) to restore the energy lost or damaged. S/He who damages or loses anything is responsable for restoring that thing. Without such accountability, without the restoration of energy, responsability does not exist. (The violation of this principle destroys any system.)

Accountability is not punishment. The restoration of energy is not to be confused with punishment. Punishment is Negative Energy designed to make bad-and-wrong and to hurt, to Cause pain to the offender, either as vengeance or so that s/he does not repeat that behavior. Restoration is the production of Positive Energy by the responsable subject to restore damage done. The restoration of damages is Accountability.

Situation:

You are a manager at an office supply company and have committed to deliver 10,000 binders to a print shop for a major job to be sent out on Friday. Your commitment calls for delivery no later than Tuesday of that week. You find out that the binders cannot be delivered until Thursday and even that is not guaranteed. There is no time for your client to find another supplier.

Victim: You explain to your client that there was a production snafu and you tried as hard as you could but it couldn't be done and besides, no one would have been able to meet that request anyway. You ask them to renegotiate with their client.

Creator: You explain the situation to your client. You ask them to arrange for a meeting with their client so you can personally explain the situation. You negotiate a new date and pick up all additional costs for your inability to meet your commitment. In addition, you offer a 20% discount on the next order.

7. **Responsability is a counterpart of Freedom.** Personal Freedom requires Responsability; Responsability does not exist in the absence of Freedom. Freedom is bounded by where that exercise of liberty unjustly

impinges on another's rights or liberty. Therefore, for freedom to work, each person must be responsable for the negative effects of his acts on others and avoid transgressions to others. With such personal responsability, that person's acts must be restrained and he loses freedom.

If a person is not free to act (to be Cause), but is under the coercion (at the Effect) of another, the responsability is with him who controls, who has the Power.

Situation:

Theresa manages a team of 30 employees. Theresa follows employees to the rest room, requires daily reporting (while other managers in the same department require weekly reporting), micro-manages all aspects of the work group and publicly humiliates employees with yelling and insults. Over the years she has had numerous grievances and harassment suits filed against her. With the last one, Theresa was told by her boss to cease and desist as he no longer had the time to deal with these continuing escalations. Theresa has unwillingly backed off directly acting out her negative behaviors, not of choice and the desire to empower (grow) her team, but by coercion. She now requires her supervisors to micro-manage all activities and report back to her. Morale and motivation remain low.

8. **Responsability is the point of transition between Cause and Effect** on the Cause-Effect Polarity Spectrum. The negation of Responsability automatically puts the person in Effect = Victim. Recognition of

Responsability opens the person to Cause.

For Theresa, change will come when she accepts Responsability for her negative behavior and begins to deal with her own Negative Emotional energies. By accepting Responsability for her emotions and behaviors Theresa begins the recovery process of moving to Cause.

More on the Condition of Victim:

The opposite polarity of Responsability → Cause vs. Effect → Victim. A victim is a person who assigns Cause for negative experiences or results to an external agent: A person who denies responsability for anything s/he FEELs, THINKs, DOes, or HAVEs, including anything that "happens to happen" to her/him. A Victim denies responsability both as the original Cause of a situation; and as being able to respond, to stop, avoid or remedy the negative effects. Victims therefore believe that life or others are doing things to them without their participation (Cause); and furthermore, that they have no ability (Cause = Power) to stop or avoid those things. Victim is a condition of self-negation of <u>Cause = Power.</u>

The Denial of Responsability Creates Victim.

Responsability is Cause: The ability to act. To deny responsability for something, you must assign that Responsability/ Cause/ Power to somebody or something else. In other words, you assign

Cause / Power to external agents. If you are not Cause, then you must be Effect, a condition of No-Power. To deny Responsability = Cause = Power in you and assign that Cause = Power to Others, is to automatically assign yourself the role of Effect = No Power. To deny Responsability is to give away your Personal Power.

On denying Responsability = Cause, you create yourself as Victim of the agent whose Cause = Power you created when you assigned it to that agent. When you blame somebody else, you are giving away your Power; you are saying that that person is more powerful than you are.

The "standard" behaviors of a Victim include:

Complain: Instead of taking action, the Victim just complains about the bad things—to anyone who will listen, but seldom to the person who could do something about it.

Blame: Assign Cause to others for the bad things in the Victim's life. Makes others "bad and wrong" for anything "bad" in the Victim's life.

Guilting[19]: Attempts to make others feel guilty for being the Causes of bad things.

Provoke and Deny having done so: The Victim by his actions, often irritates and provokes others, be that provocation deliberate or unconscious. Easily and constantly provoked, the Victim is emotionally reactive, is easily triggered and activated by others. The Victim takes no responsability for their emotions, and blames circumstances, others and external events for their pain.

---

19 Guilting: To try to make somebody feel bad for something they did; to try to put a "guilt trip" on them. The purpose of guilting someone is usually to punish them and/or manipulate them.

Low Cause in all forms: Low responsability, initiative, creativity, resourcefulness, and production.

Wait and Hope that things will get better: With or without complaining– instead of taking action.

Manipulation: Tries to get others to take action to remedy the things s/he doesn't like. Will use violations of Integrity such as lying or cheating to manipulate people and situations to get what s/he wants.

The Victim will also wave the flag of incapacity and helplessness to attract and justify getting energy from others to help them through life.

Where they can, for example, from relatives, Victims will claim duty, obligation, and debt to get energy from others. "Look at what I have done for you, how much I sacrificed: you owe me!"

As you can see, what you will get from Victims is very low positive Cause and lots of Negative Energy or Negative Cause. Victims are not Powerful people, except in the generation of Negative Energy that not only damages Group Energy Systems but ruins their personal life as well.

Now, look around at the groups of which you are a member. Look at your spouse, family, departments, community, your business—Are there any Victims running around loose?

Now, take a long, hard look at yourself: where are you demonstrating any of the characteristics of Victim?

Self-Esteem, Happiness and Responsability:

Self-esteem is your subconscious evaluation, your estimation, your good opinion of yourself. Your self-esteem depends on whether that evaluation is positive or negative. The most powerful factor in your evaluation of yourself is your perception of your Personal Power.

Your Personal Power is your ability as Cause; it is your perception of yourself as able and competent to handle life, as capable of reaching your goals. You are "good" and therefore self-love-able when you are able and powerful. You are "bad" and consequently in Negative Emotional Energy to self when you are unable, not powerful.

As Responsability is Cause, the ability to respond, to be powerful, is an essential factor in self-esteem. Denial of Responsability puts a person in Victim; Victim is a position of low Cause-Power and therefore of very poor self-esteem. Denial of Responsability/Cause/Power is directly antagonistic to your basic Nuclear Energy of Power. There is no remedy to the unhappiness of the Negative Nuclear Anti-Power IDentities and corresponding low self esteem without exiting Victim by taking Responsability.

When Others Cause Me Bad Things:

Even when others are the Cause of Negative Energy in your life, you are response-able. You may be responsable that they treated you that way (in the condition of Provoke and Deny)—or you may not. However, you are responsable for how you handle and respond to their Negative Energy. In every situation in your life, you are Cause or you are Effect. It is your declaration or denial of your Responsability that determines your condition of

Cause or Victim– not what the other person did.

Ask the question: "Who is vulnerable; who is going to suffer the effects?" That is the person it behooves to respond (take responsability) and act to avoid or change those effects, no matter who is causing the effects. In other words, the greater importance in your life is not what Other did, but rather your response: how are you going to handle (your Cause) in response to what s/he did (their Cause)? Your Cause starts with your Responsability, your recognition that unless you are chained to a post, you are at Cause over everything in your life. And if you are chained to a post, it may or may not be your responsability for getting chained to the post, but it certainly is to get unchained. To deny responsability is to give away your Cause and your Personal Power no matter what the situation or how it came to be.

It matters not what anyone did to you; That is did and done. What matters is what you do with what they did to you. What does not kill me, makes me stronger.

—NIETZSCHE

Dilution of Responsability:

Your responsability in a situation is independent of, irrelevant to, the responsability of others. To say that others are also responsable is to try to dilute or deny your own responsability.

Distortions of Responsability:

- Responsability is not obligation and burden.
- It is not Blame or Guilting.

- It does not involve bad or wrong.
- It never involves Punishment, only Accountability and replacement of energy lost.

Obligation and Burden: Responsability is felt as obligation or burden when:

1. The person is at the Effect of his Nuclear Anti-Power IDentities and so BE-FEELs that he cannot fulfill the responsability —that he will fail.
2. The additional responsability is added to his list against his will – and usually with an Accountability (offsetting Positive Energy = Reward) for him.

Thus, many people have a negative perception of responsability. However, Responsability is not these: It is a condition of Power and a person who is not at the Effect of Anti-Power IDentities or the unjust imposition of others always welcomes it.

Blame and "Guilting" versus Responsability:

Blame is "invalidation for failed Cause." Blame and Guilting imply that what the other person did is "bad and wrong"; and therefore the person is bad and wrong for having done that. This attacks self-esteem and triggers the Negative Nuclear IDentities of Anti-Power (failure) and Anti-Value (unworthy); and the accompanying Negative Emotions such as guilt, sadness, and fear. Blame and guilt are Negative Energies and so will be resisted. They damage the self-esteem of children and must never be used with children. Most of us were raised in an environment of blame and guilt. Without the ability to understand and discreate Negative Quantum Energies the work place is filled with persons with damaged self-esteem.

Responsability is just "acknowledgement of Cause." Responsability is totally free of judgments of "bad and wrong". It operates in SPace, the absence of Negative Energy: no bad and wrong, no punishment, no pain involved.

Blame uses Punishment. Responsability uses Consequences.

Punishment versus Consequences: The purpose of punishment is to hurt the other person in the hopes that s/he will refrain from the behavior in the future to avoid more pain. It likewise implies "bad and wrong." Punishment is Negative Energy and so people will resist it.

Consequences are the natural or agreed to results of a failed action. The purpose of Consequences is to remedy the negative results of actions. Consequences are the reposition of energy lost or damaged; they are part of Accountability. Thus, they are a generation of Positive Energy to repair or correct a negative situation. Consequences have no intention to cause pain; they are only to mend what did not work to produce the desired result. Thus, Responsability works hand in hand with Accountability. Accountability is being responding, being response-able, for the results of one's actions by restoring the damage or energy lost.

Responsability says, "Thank you for acknowledging that you did that. You can see that did not work to produce the desired results here (The action was Anti-Power). What do you need to do to redo/ undo / fix / replace that to make it as we agreed, or to meet the standards?" (Of course, it can be more complicated than this, but the principle stands.)

People, especially children, instinctively understand the difference between Blame → Punishment and Responsability → Consequences. People have an instinctive sense of Justice (at least while children), and naturally understand Consequences as their duty under love and fairness to repair what they damaged. Blame → Punishment is purely Negative Energy that destroys the Positive Energy-love of Responsability → Accountability. People resist Blame → Punishment; they respond positively to Responsability → Accountability.

RESPONSABILITY IS GOOD!

What people don't understand due to all the confusions we have just covered is that Responsability is something very positive. To play the game of life, you must be Cause. To win, you must be a Power-ful player. Cause-Power has a switch that turns it on and off. The on position of that switch is Responsability. The off position is Deny Responsability – which sends you into Victim.

Responsability is recognition that "I am Cause".

It is to stop assigning cause outside of myself and retake it within me. Responsability is to recognize that: "If it's to be, it's up to me."

How to take Responsability:

There is nothing to take: you already have it. You are and always have been response-able. You are the main Cause in your life. If you believe that you are not responsable, you are responsable for that belief. If you believe that you are not Cause and

Creator of your life, then you are responsable for that belief. That belief may blind you to your responsability, but does not change the fact of its existence. If you are a Victim, you are the only person responsable for creating yourself as a Victim

If you have been living denying your responsability in any area of your life (e.g. your emotions, your relationships, your career); you are responsable for denying it and trying to live as if you were not responsable. Your denial of responsability has powerful effects on your life, including the inability to change things, which will generate many, many Negative Emotions (UPS)[20] including desperation and depression. You are the sole Cause of those Effects (including UPS) by creating yourself as having no responsability. There is no way you can escape Responsability. So you see, you do not have to create Responsability, you just have to wake up to what already is.

However, if you want to adopt the point of view that you must create Responsability or yourself as Responsable; well, you can create it at any moment. It is easy. You can create your Responsability from nothing, just with your declaration that you are responsable.

This seems too easy? Notice that that is exactly how you created your no-responsability: You simply denied Responsability and assigned it to Other. Simple as that. The idea that you are not responsable is just an idea, a belief. All ideas and beliefs are your creations.

The Absolute Necessity of Responsability in the Organization:

You need Positive Cause generating Positive Energy for your organization to prosper. It is impossible to get positive results while you and your employees are operating in No-Responsability = Victim. Everyone must begin to be Responsable for:

---

20 UPS: Unhappiness, Pain & Suffering

- **Their Negative Emotions.** You and your team must stop blaming others as the cause of their emotions, and then attacking them. To realize that others are only triggers for Negative Nuclear IDentities (NIRs), and that in fact, others are doing them a favor by showing them where growth is necessary in order to polish BEing by discreating NIRs.
- **Dumping their Negative Energies (Emotions) on others.** People in no-responsability for their energies walk around spewing their anger, frustrations, anxiety, resentment, hate, feelings of inferiority, ego, complaints, blame and guilt, etc. on others and into the energy climate. All of these Negative Energies are what contaminates the energy climate of the Group Energy System. We are never justified in dumping our internal garbage on others. Our Negative Energies should be handled "in house", within ourselves.
- **The Results of Communication.** There is a law in communication that says, "The meaning of your communication is the response that you get. If you want a different response, vary your communication until you get your desired response." A person in responsability for effective communication will try different forms of communication until s/he gets the response and relation that s/he seeks. A person in no-responsability will keep communicating the same way and just keep blaming the other person for not responding right.
- **The Quality of their Relationships:** Everyone

must stop blaming others for poor relationships—problems and conflicts in their relations with others. A Victim (anybody who denies Responsability) always assigns the Cause of the problems in his relationships to the other person. He is always the innocent party. A person in responsability says "Given that I am responsable for the quality of my relationships, I need to look at what I am doing that I am getting (Causing) this reaction from others. What can I vary in my behavior (be Cause) to minimize these problems. We will later see the various mechanisms that cause poor relationships. People need to understand these mechanisms so that they can be response-able, At Cause over them.

- **Their personal results in producing what is wanted and needed in their job.** How well are the people in your organization performing in being response-able (At Cause) for the quantity and quality of their results in producing the objectives of their position in the organization? How high is their initiative, creativity, and resourcefulness? How easily do they let even slight problems serve as an excuse for not producing a result? Are they powerhouses that lets nothing get in their way? Or are they more like slugs, slow-moving, low results, and easily stopped by any problem or obstacle?

- **Responsability for the Results of their team and department.** How well do you and your team take responsability for the results of the department? When there are problems and failures, is there finger pointing or does everyone fully realize that they are part of a team and that any failure of the team is also a personal failure of theirs? You cannot create powerful teamwork without personal responsability of each member for the results of the group. Victims are not capable of powerful results or of powerful teamwork. They will be a frequent failure point, a source of Negative Energy, and a source of frustration for other team members.

- **Responsability for the organization overall.** To what degree does everyone live in the paradigm that, "I'm not responsable for the performance and success of my organization. I just work here. They pretend to pay me well, and I pretend to work well. That's about it for me." One of the ways that you can see this level of responsability is in the amount of suggestions, participation, and contribution above and beyond the call of duty. Is everyone doing their best or just enough to get by?

There is an old saying, "There are two kinds of people in the world: those that have results, and those that have excuses." Where there is too much wasted time and energy, and excuses instead of results, the responsability, the Cause Level, is low.

Responsability is the beginning of Cause. Cause is the beginning of Power. Neither you nor your organization is going to produce greater results than it is now without increasing the Cause Level (Responsability) of its primary energy generators, the people. Nor can you eliminate the Negative Quantum Energy in the organization without the people being in a condition of understanding (knowledge) and responsability for their energy.

Moving People into Cause / Responsability:

Some people take to Responsability like ducks to water. They find in it a relief and a solution to life. They see the Power that it gives them.

Others resist Responsability, for a variety of reasons:

- Some resist because of fear, fear of not being able to fulfill it, fear of failure.
- Some do not want it because it seems more comfortable to just live blaming others to avoid having to take action themselves.
- Others flee it because they want to keep playing the Victim game to manipulate others.
- Some seem to resist it because of laziness: responsability requires action. However, the laziness is the result of no-responsability, not the Cause.

No matter what the negative attitude or resistance to Responsability, it is always based in the Negative Nuclear Anti-Power IDentities. These create the BE-FEEL of no power in life. As long as a person feels that he is low-power, he feels that he would fail at being Cause. Therefore, s/he will try to escape responsability to avoid being Failed Cause. Discreate the Anti-Power IDentities and the resistance disappears.

Summary of Laws and Principles of Responsability:
- Responsability is not blame. To place blame is the denial of Responsability.

- Complaining is a denial of Responsability.
- Responsability is not guilt: it involves no opinion of bad and wrong.
- Responsability is not obligation and is not burden.
- To identify the Responsable person in any situation, ask: Who is going to suffer the effects and has any possibility of action?

The Denial of Responsability:

- Creates the Victim
- Kills Self-esteem
- Kills Power
- Kills Initiative
- Kills Pro-activity
- Kills Creativity
- Reduces Productivity
- Kills Esteem
- Damages Relationships
- Kills Happiness
- Leads to the generation of Negative Energy and therefore to pain and suffering
- Is a delusion: You are always Response-able, including for denying Response-ability and thereby creating yourself as a Victim.

Responsability is the end of Victim and the beginning of Cause, and Cause is the beginning of Power.

CHAPTER 11

The Fatal IDentity and Its Paradigm

Now that the concepts of Cause <> Effect and Victim <> Responsability have been examined in greater detail you can understand more fully the Fatal IDentity and the resulting paradigms about life. As the Causal Sequence shows (BE → FEEL → THINK → DO → HAVE); everything in life originates in your BEing. To BE Powerful, you must BE in Responsability; likewise for you and your team. A person in Victim is not BEing powerful; in fact, is starting from the IDentity of "I Am Not Powerful; I am Effect".

The Fatal IDentity, I Am Not Cause, is a state of BEing mortal to the Power of your organization. The Fatal IDentity is total Anti-Power, and is a major virus in the old Human Operating System that you must change to improve your organization. The Fatal IDentity is probably running loose and thriving in your organization. As long as it is flourishing among employees, there is little you can do to permanently improve the Energy System of your organization because people in a condition of No Responsability will continue to generate low Cause and Negative Energy that causes negative results.

Here are some variants of the Fatal IDentity, followed by the Fatal Paradigm that results:

- Fatal IDentity: I AM NOT the cause, much less the creator, of my Emotions. (Fatal Paradigm: Therefore, you must be. You cause my emotions; you make me feel good or bad. Therefore, I must control you to be happy.)

- IDentity: I AM NOT responsable for what I feel. (Paradigm: It is your responsability to make me happy. It is your fault when I am upset and suffering. It is your duty to make me happy; you owe me that. Now obey me and BE and DO as I want you to!)

- Anti-Power IDentity: I CAN'T control my emotions. They just happen, or you caused them. (Therefore, I am justified in dumping them on you, in spraying you with my anger, invalidation and blaming. And since how I feel is your fault, I am justified in trying to make you feel bad also.)

- I AM NOT the cause and therefore not responsable for the problems in my relationships. (Paradigm: The other person is the cause of the conflicts and problems, not me. Therefore s/he must act differently; s/he must change; not I)

- I AM NOT cause and not responsable for the bad things that manifest in my life. I am the Victim here, don't you see? The only thing I can do is complain and blame, hoping somebody will do something—and I do, lots.

- I AM NOT responsable for the success or failure of my organization. I just work there.

- I AM NOT responsable for my happiness. (Paradigm: I married to have someone make me happy—although they are not doing a very good job of it. And, of course, I let them know about their failure at every opportunity with my complaints, criticism and blaming. They have got to change and start making me happy.)

- I AM NOT responsable for my addictions. My parents (or society or whatever) did it to me. I am their Victim. I have no control over what they did to and made of me. Isn't that tragic?

- "The Devil made me do it." (or whatever other external agent that is assigned Cause; could just as well be little voices in my head or dancing angels or sugar plum fairies).

And on and on: it is impossible to list all the things for which people deny Cause and Responsability. Any time you see somebody complaining; anytime you see anybody blaming anybody or anything for something in her life; you are staring their Fatal IDentity in the face.

THINK

The Fatal IDentity and its Paradigm are flaws in the THINK of a person. Continuing on in our exploration of the Causal Sequence brings us to the next element of life, THINK, also known as the mind. The mind is very powerful, but that power works both ways. In one hand, it holds the sword of Reason and Knowledge that gives us the power of today's science and technology. We owe all the ease and comforts of modern life to the mind. However, on the other hand, it is a dagger that destroys your happiness, and damages and kills your relationships.

You have already seen in the Fatal IDentity that you are not the creator of your emotions, and therefore not the creator of your happiness <> suffering. The Fatal Paradigm is: Given that you are not Cause (the Fatal IDentity), then externals, something outside of myself, must be – and away you go on the impossible External Quest of trying to control the world to stop your pain and be happy. As long as you are operating in the Fatal IDentity → Fatal Paradigm → External Quest sequence, happiness is impossible. The best you can do is MOPs, and these always wear off because they do not involve any real change in your BEing and therefore in your FEELing (happiness).

We have spoken of the general reactivity of people to events, and how they let events trigger their Negative Nuclear IDentities and therefore their Negative Emotions. What makes all this even worse, is that in general, people are not reacting to events, to What is, to Reality! They are reacting to and being triggered on their created distortions about Reality, on their illusions.

If you understand the mind and how it distorts Reality by creating illusions, delusions, and mirages, so that you can stop reacting to all of these; you will take a giant step into SPace, serenity, and "peace of mind".

To begin, "Truth" must be defined. Truth is the opposite of illusions, delusions, mirages, opinions, judgments, beliefs, speculations, stories, and manipulations.

Truth

Definition: Truth is the degree of verifiable correspondence, of agreement, between a reality (thing or event) and a statement about that reality. To the degree that a statement precisely represents the reality it is describing, it is Truth.

Truth in this book will always be capitalized to signify its importance, both as something powerful for humanity (the basis of science, technology, and power) and as a reminder of the full and specific definition of the concept.

If there is correspondence, then Truth exists. If the statement does not correspond to the reality; if it does not accurately represent the reality, then the statement is not Truth. If there is no way to verify that correspondence, the statement likewise cannot be certified as Truth.

"Truth" is a label of certification of the absolute quality, the absolute dependability and reliability of a statement. Truth is something you can stake your life on. This means that if the reality you are speaking of is not available to verify the accuracy of the statement so that the correspondence is not verifiable, it is not known; then that statement is not Truth. Whether it is True or not is unknown, unverified, and it may not be declared Truth. Any statement without proof is merely an opinion, a belief, a point of view.

Just The Facts, Ma'am.

Another name for "Truth" is "the facts". "Just the facts, ma'am", is a famous saying ascribed to the classic detective show, Dragnet. To get to the real facts, to the Truth, you must eliminate personal opinions, beliefs, hearsay and all other unsupported ideas. This is why courts and trials have such rigorous procedural and evidence rules.

Science

Truth is also the purpose of science. The scientific method is a rigorous system designed to filter through every plausible idea and hypothesis to find the best available explanation of phenomena; those statements that best correspond to how events occurs. (This is the best Truth available –Truth will change as new data comes in.) Before science, all that mankind had were hundreds of thousands of superstitions, fantasies, legends, and myths about how the universe worked.

One and Universal

Because Truth is based on verifiable evidence, on proof, such that all rational people must agree that it is so; Truth is always one and universal. It is always the one and the same Truth and all people subscribe to it. A good example of this is the physical sciences–physics, chemistry or biology. they are one and the same over the globe and everybody uses the same laws and formulas. There is harmony and agreement instead of arguments and conflict which will exist when there is no Truth.

Where there are notable differences between one set of ideas and another, then the Truth is not known.

Beliefs

A belief is a statement to which a person has arbitrarily assigned the label of Truth in the absence of evidence and verification. Where there is no verification there is no Truth. "Belief" is a dirty word in law, science, and philosophy. It is also deadly to your personal power in life, which is what you will see in this chapter.

The Mind: THINK in the Causal Sequence

The purpose of the mind is to create. It creates thoughts, ideas, hypotheses, solutions to problems, art, designs, planes, machines, etc. When these are accurate reflections of reality, of events –Truth–our mind creations are useful to create and control the physical universe. That creation and control is Power. Thus, the mind is our source of Power over the universes, both the external and our internal world (once you understand this book). But what the mind does is create. And, if you don't understand it and control it, it will create a lot of junk and garbage. Remember GIGO: Most people think that what is in their mind, what they THINK is the truth. This is very seldom true. Much of all human THINKing are distortions of reality; are illusions and delusions. Many people live far too much in their head, in a fantasy world or their own making. The failure to understand the difference between Truth, the Facts, and these created distortions causes an infinity of problems, conflicts, and suffering.

Here is a listing of the some of the common distortions:

The Mind

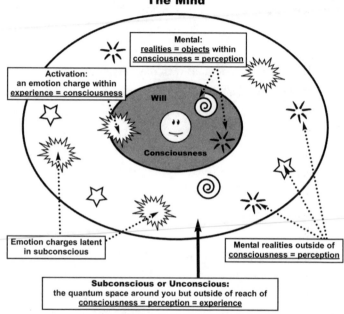

Interpretations and Meanings: An event occurs. A person seeing that event then creates all kinds of interpretations of the event, and assigns meanings to the event and intentions to other people involved. For example, one person enters a room and does not say hello to one or more persons, or even to all. Some people will interpret that to mean that the person entering does not like or wants to slight the person(s) not greeted.

This is an interpretation, the creation of a meaning. We have no idea the significance of that behavior unless we ask the person doing it. For example, I won't greet people on entering a room if I see they are concentrating on something or talking to others, in order to avoid interrupting them. The Truth, the fact, is that the person did not greet everybody, and that is all that we truly know. Anything else is speculation.

We see this all the time in relationships where one spouse interprets the other's behavior, usually negatively. For example, when a person is jealous (which is always caused by Anti-Value Nuclear IDentities) interpretations of even minuscule events can serve as triggers for the jealousy and the resulting fights. In organizations, some people attentively watch the boss for any sign of favoritism or of slight, ready to interpret totally innocent actions as for or against them. The same works in reverse as often the manager will look for these same signs and assign incorrect interpretations as well.

Personalization: This is similar to interpretations, but adds the creation that an event is deliberately committed against the interpreter. Somebody does something, and the other person takes it personally, as intended to slight or insult him. However, the only reason anybody takes anything personally and gets activated about it, is because the event activated their Negative Nuclear IDentities. For example, if somebody calls you stupid, and you get upset, it is because that is triggering your subconscious Anti-Wisdom IDentities. If you know you are smart, if you BE-FEEL it, somebody calling you stupid has no effect on you.

Taking things personally is the result of a creation of personal importance. We create personal importance to compensate our Anti-Value Nuclear IDentities. A person who lives in Value Nuclear IDentities does not need assurance of their worth and value from external sources, and so is impervious to the detractions of others. S/he is the generator of their BE-FEEL of Value, not externals; and is able to hold their BE-FEEL of Value-able in the face of all counter-opinions.

Here is a secret: Nothing other people do or say is ever about you. Nothing. Even when they attack you directly with epithets, spewing anger and venom; they are only activated and acting at the Effect of their NIRs, projecting their IDentities on you (to try to escape them) and venting their own pain. (Projection and escape are discussed in Chapter 12.)

Externals never cause your experience. Nothing of what anybody ever says to you or how they treat you has any effect on you unless you give it that power, unless you import it into your world and believe in it. Why import others' NIRs and emotional garbage? —Don't you have enough of your own to deal with? So never take anything personally. It's not personal; and even if it were, it has no power other than that which you give it.

Stories and Histories: An event occurs. The facts are usually simple and direct. However, some people take the event and spin a long story around it. Usually they are both the Innocent Victim and the Hero/Heroine, making the other person the bad guy, the wrong or stupid one (more Projection is used to escape).

The best examples of "Stories and Histories" you will find in your own life. Who delights in telling you long stories about something that happened in the past –sometimes years ago? They will also tell the story in present tense, present verb time, and blow by blow. Furthermore, they will tell you the same story over and over again, at intervals of days or weeks or months, as if you had never heard it before. Know anybody like that?

The same thing happens in organizations. Many enterprises go out of business as they glorify days gone by when they were 'the best game in town'. While the leadership and ranks bask in the glories of days long gone, the rest of the world moved on.

Programs: A Program is a mental overlay of how another

person should or should not be. The purpose of the program is to control externals so that they comply with our ideas of how they should be—so that we can avoid the activation of Negative IDentities or activate positive ones.

To see programs at work, simply ask yourself who in your life is trying to specify or dictate to you any aspect of how you should live? That is their programs about you. When the other person fails to comply with your programs, you activate a Negative IDentity and often attack the person with invalidation and anger. Remember that your own Negative Emotional energy is the only pain and suffering that exists. You are the first person to suffer that energy.

The purpose of the Negative Energy attack is to stop or change the other person to comply with the program. The subconscious cause of the Negative Energy is always a Negative Nuclear IDentity. The programming person is subconsciously trying to control his/her BE-FEEL (IDentities) by controlling the other person.

Programs are one of the fundamental problems in relationships. They are intents to dictate the BE, FEEL, THINK, DO, or HAVE of others in order to achieve one's own happiness. Programs are always a denial of freedom to others to create for themselves life as they would have it. They are an invalidation of how others are, and therefore a denial of SPace, of acceptance of others as they are.

Notice who in your life is programming you, trying to dictate to you how you should BE, FEEL, DO. Notice how you react to their insistences. You do not accept that others control you therefore, how can you expect them to allow you to control them?

Programs are delusions. Nobody can ever know how you should BE or what you should DO. Likewise, you can never know how another person should BE → FEEL → THINK →DO → HAVE, much less be justified in attacking him or her with your Negative Energy to get them to comply.

Programs at Work

Visions versus Program: You have visions. A vision is a mental image of how you would like something to be in the future. It starts from a condition of acceptance of how things are now. Instead of resisting the present situation with Negative Energy as programs do; a vision focuses on creating a desirable future using Positive Energy. A program will put you in to re-sistance of What Is. A vision emotionally accepts What Is and motivates Positive Energy and action for the future.

Between programs and visions, there is a huge difference in how you focus and use energy. However, you can not impose your visions on others, only communicate them. In order for businesses and organizations to be successful, leaders and executives must become adept in communicating visions to everyone in the system. The vision must be shared by the CEO throughout the organization, all the way to the mailroom clerk.

Good and Bad: Pay careful attention. The information in this section can lead you to a life of power, wisdom and integrity. What do you consider 'good' and what do you consider 'bad'?

Please note that in this book, 'bad' does not refer to real and bad events where there is verifiable, true harm or damage to others; or where ethical, moral, or legal codes are violated. We are referring to the opinions of 'bad' that we create every day in life as it unfolds around us, about other people and situations around us. To see these, make a list of your activations (of Negative Emotions). Now make a list of your trigger events: what other people do and say, and simply what occurs in life. Are any of those trigger events bad in the sense that they violate a moral law? Very few, right? The vast majority are just other people being themselves and life unfolding as it unfolds.

For example: That person that cut you off in traffic, or out of that parking space. You think that was bad, but to him it was good. No moral law was violated; the cards just fell his way that time. This is an example of something that is not a bad event except as you have created it to be in your mind.

Another example: Somebody calls you an idiot. Is that bad? Not at all. It is somebody expressing her opinion exercising her rights of free speech (and projecting her NIRs on you). However, you paint such things as bad in your mind; you thus create "bad" where it does not exist.

You have been labeling events bad because they appear to be causing you emotional pain. However, it has been shown that nothing outside of you ever causes your emotions, your suffering in life. Therefore, those events are not bad; they are just triggers. They are just life unfolding as it unfolds. Your job is to not be at the effect of that; to be able to maintain serenity no matter what happens. You do this by learning to hold your Positive Nuclear IDentities (and discreate the Negative IDentities when they do activate.)

There is a lot of "bad" in your life, and you are the sole creator of it – unless it actually violates some code or law. All these judgments of "bad" are another form of our mental hallucinations. Now let's look at the other side of that.

Your Negative Emotions are always resistance to "bad" things and events. You celebrate good events and resist bad ones. (Actually, as you now know, they are really resistance and Negative Energy directed to your "bad" self, to your Negative Nuclear IDentities. This is explained further below.) Your own Negative Emotions are the only pain and suffering that exist in your life. You are the creator of your opinions of bad. You create the distortion that someone or something is bad, and then you resist the "bad" event with Negative Emotional energy that is your pain. Thus, by creating events as bad and then emotionally resisting them, you create your pain in life. You do it all, alone! You are the Creator!

Law: It is impossible to suffer without first having created bad.

Your Negative Emotions = Pain are really your resistance to your "bad" self, to your Negative Nuclear Identities (Anti-Wisdom, Anti-Power, Anti-Value.) What you really create as "bad" is your self in your NIRs. It is your resistance to your self in those "bad"

IDentities that activates your Negative Emotions=Pain. The externals only serve to trigger the IDentities.

Furthermore, that triggering only happens because you are not controlling your IDentities, as you should be. You are living letting the world choose who you are according to the circumstances of the moment. You are letting yourself bounce up and down and around in your Nuclear IDentity Polarities according to whatever is happening around you. You are living At Effect of the world, instead of At Cause over your Self.

When a person doesn't understand all this, then s/he assigns or projects Cause of Negative Emotions to the trigger. S/He then paints the trigger event as "bad", as the apparent cause of emotional pain. We have proven that externals never cause your pain; thus they are technically never bad for causing pain. When you project "bad" onto events where it does not exist objectively; you become the Creator of Bad.

All of this is part of the Fatal IDentity–I am not Cause of my experience. This leads to the Fatal Paradigm–therefore, externals must be Cause (the External Quest). Caught in the External Quest, THINK becomes, "I must stop the 'bad' things that trigger my Negative Emotions. However, the fatal "bad" you are creating is not so much to externals, as it is to your Self where you have created your Self as NIRs.

It is a great achievement when you learn to look at your Self, at your Negative Nuclear IDentities, without your creations of bad. That is the beginning of your SPace to your Self to BE as you are, and as you are not. That SPace for yourself is the beginning of Love for Self, the beginning of true positive self-esteem. Your NIRs are not bad; they are just creations. Your "bads" are likewise just your mental creations (delusions, actually). Your

NIRs are just the negative polarity of the Nuclear or Life Essence Energy of which you are made.

You resist your NIRs with Negative Emotion, because you have created them as bad. That resistance to Self is your only pain in life, and it causes the persistence of the Negative IDentities. Were you to accept them / you as they/you are, they would discreate and you would automatically flip back to the Positive IDentities. You get stuck in the Negative IDentities because you resist them, and Resistance Causes Persistence. You resist them because you painted them "bad." Remember, they are not "bad". They are a natural and essential part of your spirit and your existence, because you are made of the Nuclear Life Energy of Wisdom, Power, Value and Joy and that energy is a polarity.

Understand this: You create your NIRs "bad"; you then resist them with your Negative Emotions; you then suffer your resistance, which you then blame on the triggers, and so paint them "bad". Meanwhile, your resistance causes persistence of your NIRs, and makes them appear even more real and stronger and more painful; so you paint them even "badder" and resist them even more, so you have more pain, and more persistence—and around and around and down you go!

You do it all! You create all your pain and suffering in life and you create it because of your mental creation of "bad" about your Negative Nuclear IDentities. Your negative, painful emotions are your Resistance to your NIRs and they are the only Unhappiness, Pain & Suffering that exist.

More on "Bad"

One of the definitions of "bad" is that which causes pain.

Nothing external ever causes you emotional pain, so nothing external is ever bad for that reason (as opposed to causing real harm or damage or violating a code.) One place we create a lot of "bad" is when other people don't obey our programs of how they should or should not be. Other people have no duty to obey your programs, nor do you, theirs.

Every person is Cause over his or her internal energies. Events can only be triggers for the Negative Nuclear IDentities and controlling our NIRs is the sovereign province and responsability of each person. You cannot expect to control the world to control your IDentities – you have to do that yourself, internally. The world will not, nor does the world have any responsability to conform to your ideas of how it should be (obey your programs) so we can walk around in Positive IDentities (BE-FEEL) and be happy.

Just because a person is triggered by what others do, does not mean that what those others are doing is wrong or bad. Others are not violating a moral or legal code, only exercising their right of choice to BE and DO as they wish, rather than according to the programs of someone else. They have no duty to curtail their freedoms just because another person doesn't approve and becomes activated.

You are not harming anyone just because they get activated because you don't fulfill their programs and expectations. If you, while exercising your rights of freedom to be you, trigger the NIRs of others, that is their problem, not yours. They will make you bad and wrong for triggering their NIRs, but you cannot live your life according to their programs and expect to find your own happiness. They are dumping their Negative Energy on you trying to control you so that you obey their programs to make them happy – at the expense of your own happiness.

As long as you are not actively projecting Negative Energy on others, and as long as you are pursuing your legitimate rights to freedom and to seek your happiness; the activations of others is their problem. Their activations are their ignorance and lack of control of their IDentities, and their efforts to control their IDentities by controlling the external world, you in this case. Their activations are their emotional fits trying to control you, as a three-year old does his parents.

Likewise, others are not "bad", just because they don't obey your programs, or just because they trigger you.

You have no duty or obligation to sacrifice your happiness for the happiness of others. To begin with, that is impossible: you cannot make another person happy. The best you can do is:

1) Provide a MOP (Moment of Pleasure): Fleetingly activate his or her PIRs (giving gifts, obeying his programs) often at the cost of sacrificing your own preferences and happiness in the situation. You can achieve your happiness only by following your own instincts for your BE → FEEL → THINK → DO → HAVE. If you sell out to pressures from others (such as their activations toward you) you can say good-bye to your happiness.

2) Tiptoe on eggshells around him or her, obeying his or her every wish to try to avoid triggering his or her NIRS – something that is also fundamentally impossible.

Not only is it impossible to make others happy, but also you have no duty or obligation to try. You do not have the power to make them happy, and their happiness is not your responsability (Where you have no power, you can have no responsability). You have your hands full trying to achieve your own happiness. It is impossible for you to achieve your happiness making your life revolve around the happiness of others. You cannot achieve your happiness selling out[21] your BE → FEEL → THINK → DO →HAVE to obey, to comply with the BE → FEEL → THINK →DO → HAVE of others for you (their programs for you).

Moreover, their ideas of BE→FEEL→THINK→ DO→ HAVE for you are designed for their happiness, not yours. Their programs are their ideas for you that will make them happy, not you. It is impossible for one person to know the highest, the ideal Causal Sequence for another person. It is arrogance to think that you do, even if speaking of your own children, or members of your organization.

Life begins to work when:

1) You stop selling yourself out to fulfill the programs of others, to give them MOPs or avoid their MODs[22] (activations); and

2) You stop demanding of others that they fulfill your programs, and give them the freedom to choose their own BE →FEEL → THINK → DO → HAVE.

---

21 Definition: to sell yourself out. To put the programs, demands, priorities of others above your own such that you must sacrifice what you want in the name of making others happy. This is a huge paradigmatic trap in which many people live.

22 MODs are Moments of Dolor. Moments of Pain, an experience of Unhappiness. The opposite of a MOP.

You only try to dictate their lives as part of your External Quest to control externals to control your Nuclear IDentities. You are learning to control your IDentities directly – thus, you can let the world be as it may be. You don't need it to be in any particular way for you to be happy. You are happy because you are in the BE-FEEL of the Positive Nuclear IDentities – this is the only happiness that exists.

It is not the duty of the organization, or you as a leader, to make your people happy – and that is impossible anyway. However, you are paying the price of their unhappiness in the form of all the Negative Energy they are injecting into the Organization Energy System. Therefore, it behooves you to teach your employees these things so that they can take Responsability for their energies and relations, and so stop the generation of the Negative Energy.

As long as they don't know, they will continue to generate Negative Energy, programs and "bads" and the entire Energy System pays the price. It may not be fair, but that is the way it is.

Here is a list of some of the delusions that we have seen so far in this book. Any of these seem familiar? (Some are stated more than once to capture the point of view from both sides of its polarity).

- I am not Cause. I am not the Creator of my IDentities, thoughts, emotions, and relationships.
- I am not responsable.
- I am a Victim.
- Externals control my Quantum experience, especially my emotions.

- External events (triggers) cause my pain and suffering.
- Some day, if only I can identify, accumulate, and hoard enough of the right things, externals will make me happy.
- All interpretations and assigned meanings to events.
- Personalizations: All personalizations of events.
- Stories and histories.
- Programs: "should / should not be", especially as to how others should or should not be, but also includes how events that have already happened should have been. (Once something is, it is: "should have been" is another delusion.)
- "Bads"—other than the ones that cause actual physical harm or damage.*

  * It is critical that you understand that nobody is "bad" just because they activate somebody else; they are not thereby causing someone harm or pain. There is no such thing as causing Quantum damage to someone – we have proved that externals never cause Quantum experience, and that each BEing is Cause over his or her internal energies. Events can only be triggers for the Negative Nuclear IDentities and controlling our NIRs is the sovereign province and responsability of each person. You cannot expect to control the world to control your IDentities – you have to do that yourself, internally. The world will not, nor does the world have any responsability to, conform to your ideas of how it should be (obey your programs) so you can walk around in Positive IDentities (BE-FEEL) and be happy.

Law: You can't control Reality by dealing with illusions:

How can you expect to control reality and Life, and achieve happiness, if you are living in such delusions? How can you expect your organization to function at peak performance levels when its members are ignorant of the mental realities that they create?

Polarization:

Most of these delusions lead to Polarization. Polarization is the division of anything into two groups, one of which is the in-crowd, the "good" guys; and the other is the out-group, the "bad" guys. According to the good guys, the bad guys should not BE / THINK / DO as they are or do. Do not confuse Polarization with Polarity. Polarities are naturally occurring Energy Spectrums making possible degrees and scales of experience. Polarization is uniquely a human creation, one of the delusions of the uncontrolled mind. It is related to "should/should not be", programs, created "bads", and other such mental images.

Polarization occurs where a person creates (thereby interpreting and distorting Reality) that other people are inferior, less than, bad, or wrong. Globally this separation is usually based on superficial and insignificant differences such as race, ethnicity, nationality, sexual orientation, economic status, gender, politics or religion. By polarizing people on such insignificant things, and often on things over which the out-group has no control (such as gender, nationality, race); the in-group gets to declare itself superior, better and more deserving, without having to compete on ability and merit.

In many companies you can observe polarization as:

Management —Union
Management — Non-Union Associates
Office Personnel — Outside Technicians
Salaried Employees — Hourly Employees

Polarization even occurs within families. Examine feuds within families and more often than not you will find family members 'taking sides' often on issues of little significance. It is the sad history of humankind that polarization is so prevalent. Look at your organization and at the world: is there much polarization in your organization? Is there polarization of humanity?

We can see that polarization exists in every corner of the world. Humanity is polarized in nations, races, politics, religions, cultures – name a difference and you can find polarization. How many problems and conflicts is polarization causing in your organization?

What polarization particularly ignores is that we are all Life Energy, spiritual entities; BEings made of exactly the same Nuclear Life Energy, of the basic and One Life Energy we abbreviate as Wisdom, Power, Value, and Emotion.

Summary

- What Is, Is. What ain't, ain't.
- Your pain is never Reality, but your resistance to Reality, because you have painted it "bad".
- You are the creator of your "bads".
- You can not create what you want, resisting what you have.
- Once something Is, it already Is As It Is.

- It is foolish to resist Reality with Negative Energy—which is your only pain in life, and causes the persistence of that which your resist.
- Wisdom focuses Positive Energy on creating the future.

CHAPTER 12

SPace

There are three fundamental factors that you must understand and handle to control life: Cause, SPace[23], and Energy. Although mentioned briefly earlier these concepts are explained in greater detail here. To summarize what has been introduced to this point:

Energy:

Everything that exists is energy. All forms of energy fall into one of six classifications:

BE → FEEL → THINK → DO (RELATE) → HAVE

---

23 Reminder–SPace is spelled with two capital first letters to signal that a particular concept of existence, as opposed to physical space.

These operate as a **Causal Sequence** in which the elements to the left determine the following elements to the right. Of these six kinds of energy, only DO and HAVE are of the physical. The others, BE, FEEL, THINK, and the RELATE half of DO are non-physical, Quantum Energies. Note that more of life is Quantum than physical.

The Quantum Energies are also the most important things in your life. Everything in your mind, every thought, is a Quantum Energy form. Your emotions are non-physical, Quantum Energies. Your identities, including the Nuclear IDentities that are the most powerful things in your life, are energy masses. Your happiness <> suffering is purely a question of your Energies, of Positive or Negative Emotions. Your mental creations of interpretations, histories, personalizations, programs, and "bads" are all energy forms. You paint things "bad" and then resist them with your Negative Emotions and suffer that pain, while blaming it all on the reality. All of these are Quantum Energies and processes.

The Spectrum of Emotion

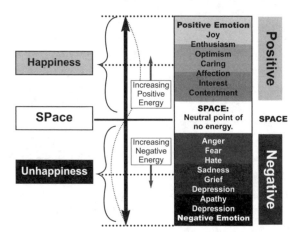

The ultimate motivation of everything you THINK and DO is to control your BE and FEEL. What you really seek in life, the ultimate motivation of all actions and behaviors, is to BE as much of the Nuclear Life Energy (Wisdom, Power, Value) as you can so that you experience as much Positive Energy as possible. It's all about energy. (As there isn't anything else, there isn't anything else it could be about.)

As your life and your organization run on all these energies, your ability to control them is critical to your personal power (your ability to produce the results you want in life), and also to the quality of your life and happiness. Your control of energy is a question of

1) Knowledge of how energy works.
2) Your level of Cause in Life.

Cause is needed to create SPace. SPace **is the key to effective and permanent control and elimination of Negative Energy.**

Cause:

To live Life At Cause is to live life from a position of power, of control of energy; as opposed to living in Effect, which is being acted upon and controlled by external agents of Cause. The condition of believing that you are Effect is called Victim. The point of transition between Cause and Effect is the recognition, the acknowledgment, of Response-ability. Response-ability and Cause are the natural states of the non-physical (spiritual) BEing that you are. You don't have to do anything to be at Cause other than to discreate your creation, your Fatal IDentity, that you are not Cause, that you are not Response-able.

This seems obvious and easy, but when we look at life, there are very few people who are living At Cause, in Response-ability, in every area of their lives.

Some people may raise their hands here with a whole list of reasons and situations where they are not Cause:

Examples:

- I can't do this because of the budget.
- I can't do this because I can't get good people. ·
- My hands are tied because of government regulations, etc.
- I want to make changes but my boss won't let me.
- I'd like to get along with my family but I'm the outcast.
- I'm unhappy in this job and would like to do something else but my wife won't let me.

Yes, you are at the effect of such things, and may not have control — if you are in Victim mentality. In a state of victimhood your responsability is reduced. To move to Cause:

1) Begin by acknowledging that you are in this situation by your own choice. Nobody made you go here or makes you continue here.
2) What does it take to stop you— to stop your Cause and Power? Given those limitations, are you being stopped where you need not be?
3) Are you in response-ability in all the areas of your life, not just your job?

SPace:

The third factor of existence needed to understand and control life is SPace. SPace is the secret ingredient to controlling Negative Energy. You cannot control Negative Energy with Negative Energy as that just piles up more Negative Energy. Remember, Resistance Causes Persistence. To define SPace:

SPace is nothingness. It is the absence of all energy (includes matter).

Just as there is physical space, which means nothing is there, so too is there Quantum SPace.

- Emotionally, SPace is the absence of activations, of all Negative Emotional energy. Therefore, it is peace and serenity.
- Mentally, SPace is the absence of all creation of the mental illusions that fill the space of our mind with our mental delusions.

Mental SPace includes the absence of our interpretations and creations of meanings that color and distort our perceptions of the facts, of the raw truth, of what really is. SPace is the absence of the creations of opinions of the Should be <> Should not be, of programs. Thus, SPace is the mental and emotional acceptance of how others are and are not, and of events as they occur. SPace is no energy and therefore acceptance of What Is, as opposed to resisting Reality with Negative Energy. From a condition of SPace, you can focus on what you prefer in the future and use Positive Energy to manifest that.

SPace is the absence of the creations of "**bad**" [24]about our triggers, events that activate your Negative Nuclear IDentities and their Negative Emotion charges. SPace knows that external events are never the cause of your suffering and therefore are never "bad" only because they trigger you. SPace is the Wisdom of understanding that life itself is a parade of events. These events are neither good nor bad, except, as Shakespeare said, "Our thinking makes it so". The wise person recognizes that the creation of opinions of "bad, wrong, and should not be" about things are just personal creations of interpretations and distortions of reality.

Mental SPace includes giving SPace to the sayings and doings of others, giving them the freedom to BE, SAY, and DO without generating Negative Energy against them. This includes being SPace to their intended slights and insults to us. **SPace never takes anything personally**, recognizing that what others say and do is always their own misguided efforts to obey the Existential Imperative in their own quest for happiness. When SPace does respond to something that somebody else says or does, it does so from serenity, self-control, and Wisdom; not from Negative Nuclear IDentities and emotional reactivity.

SPace is therefore the absence of all the mental illusions that distort reality and trigger resistance and all forms of Negative Energy to anything in life. Thus, SPace is a condition of BEing itself, of the spirit. It is the degree of Cause and Personal Power we have to be able to control all our Quantum Energies, particularly to avoid the generation of Negative Energy. Never forget that Negative Emotions are the only pain for self and others.

---

24 Remember that we are referring to our arbitrary "bads" about others and normal life, especially about our triggers, as distinguished from "bad" things where there is real harm or violations of legal or moral codes.

Scenario #1:

Your team misses its monthly objective. You are activated (anger from your Anti-Power Nuclear IDentity). Instinctively and subconsciously, you want to evade responsability. Mentally, you jump to the conclusion that not everyone is pulling their weight. Mentally, you make them wrong and bad: "My staff is lazy; they are goofing off". "My supervisors are not running the show adequately." At the effect of your activation of anger and frustration, you set up control systems to measure everyone's output, complete with mandated daily and weekly objectives for each person. People pick up on your energy of anger, control, and imposition. The result is subdued energy in the group, sabotage and production slow down.

Law: Activations destroy Wisdom.

Scenario #2:

You discharge and discreate your Anti-Power NIR until you are serene and in SPace. You then meet with your managers and key personnel and present the situation: the monthly objective was not met – and you do so without Negative Energy and without invalidation. You invite a discussion on possible causes and obtain as many viewpoints as possible. (You let their energy flow.) Once everyone is aware of all viewpoints and factors, you turn the attention and energy to the desired future state (exceeding the next objective); and to what each and all are going to do different or more to create that state. You keep the SPace open so that all can flow their best ideas (mental energies) to the plan of action. You create a group agreement on what is to happen with individual commitments from each for their part in the plan. Your team leaves understanding the situation, with a solution and plan. Their self-esteem and motivation are preserved and enhanced. You have empowered them. The difference is the energy you were handling.

As you can see, SPace is very powerful. And there is more:

SPace is the beginning of all Power to handle and discreate Negative Energy.

Resistance is to throw Negative Energy against Negative Energy, which only piles on more and more Negative Energy. SPace is no energy, no resistance; it permits the original Negative Energy to flow. This flow discharges and discreates the Negative Energy.

Law: Energy flows to SPace. Energy that flows, grows. (Here, "grows" means it moves up the Energy Frequency Spectrum from negative towards positive.)

Consider this case: Somebody comes to you activated in anger (Anti-Power IDentities) about something you did. (Yes, hard to believe that this could ever happen to you but just take it as an example.) If you become angry in return, resisting their Negative Energy with yours, what happens? Does not the Negative Energy between the two increase? However, if you just listen and let them vent, flow their Negative Energy (anger), it will began to diminish and eventually disappear. That is giving SPace to their Negative Energy (anger and their invalidations of you, in this case).

186

Another very important example of the relationship between SPace and Negative Energy occurs when you decide to discreate your Negative Nuclear IDentities. Your Negative Nuclear IDentities persist in your BEing because you have been resisting them with your creations of "bad to be that way" (e.g. It's bad that I can't do it.). Always remember that your Negative Emotions are generated around a Negative Nuclear IDentity.

If you allow SPace to your Negative Nuclear IDentities by removing your label of "bad", you will cease to resist yourself with your Negative Emotions. You are then able to move into the SPace of BEing that way (the NIR) so that you fully BE-FEEL that Negative IDentity. By allowing yourself to fully experience your Negative IDentity it will discreate and disappear. Not only will you FEEL it discreate, but you will no longer be reactive to that trigger.

SPace is the middle point, transition point, on all of the principal Quantum Energy Polarity Scales. SPace is the entry point to Positive Energy. Positive Energy is that which encourages, aids, supports, heals, builds, grows, integrates or unites things or people. As an Energy System, such as your family or company, Negative Energy is any kind of energy that discourages, retards, avoids, separates, divorces, harms, damages, or destroys things or people. (See the diagram following.)

As living in the negative scales of any of the above spectrums is contra-personal power and painful, it is unwise to do so. SPace is the end of ignorance and foolishness and the beginning of Wisdom on the Wisdom polarity scale.

SPace is the midpoint on the Resistance-Effect; SPace-Cause Polarity. It is the end of the At Effect condition caused by Resistance, and therefore the beginning of Cause and Power. You are the Effect of whatever you resist: in other words, what you resist controls you. (For one example, what you resist causes your pain.)

SPace is the mid-point on the Emotional Energy Polarity Spectrum and on the Happiness <> Pain Polarity Spectrum. (Recall that these are the same energy spectrum.) SPace is the upper end point of the Negative Emotional energy scale. SPace is the end of the Negative Emotions that are the only unhappiness, suffering and pain that exist in life. As the end and absence of the Negative Emotions, it is therefore the beginning of the Positive Emotions that are the only happiness and joy that exists.

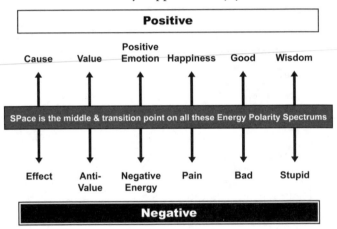

SPace as the mid-point on the Emotional Energy Polarity Spectrum.

SPace is also the key to the end of Polarization. To give SPace to others is to give them the recognition and acceptance of how they are. It is to give them the SPace to BE as they are, and to Not-BE as they are not. SPace is the absence of invalidation and resistance to the forms of BEing of others. In SPace, the differences between people of ethnicity, sexual orientation, religion are celebrated as contributing to the variety of the universe, rather than divided out from the whole to be punished or eradicated.

A Review of the Laws of Energy:

- Energy Flows to SPace.
- Negative Energy must exist for Positive Energy to exist (Law of Polarity).
- Negative Energy includes any form of Resistance to What Is BEing As It Is.

Therefore, Negative Energy is always Resistance to Reality.

- Negative Energy allowed to flow, dissipates and dis-creates, thereby ceasing to exist. Therefore, SPace dissipates Negative Energy.
- Negative Energy against Negative Energy only creates more Negative Energy. In other words; Resistance Causes More Resistance and Persistence.

There are few things in life that do so much for so many. Try putting a little SPace in your BEing, and therefore in your life, family, and organization. No real transformation of an Energy System is possible without it.

CHAPTER 13

Negative Nuclear IDentity Behaviors

B y now it should be clear that you create your life according to your Causal Sequence. Everything that occurs in your experience, in your life emanates from your Nuclear IDentities, your BE. These Quantum Energies define Who You Are in every moment of your life.

Your experience of Positive or Negative Nuclear IDentities determines your experience of Happiness or Pain. Positive IDentities lead to positive thought and action; likewise Negative IDentities lead to negative thought and action. All of these work in synergy to create what shows up for you in your physical experience, your physical universe.

All of your pain is the activation of NIR masses in your Consciousness. Your suffering is your Resistance to pain. Under the force of the Existential Imperative, in order to avoid negative experience and obtain positive experience you now know that:

The only motivation of all human behavior is one's own happiness, to avoid pain and achieve happiness.

Since happiness is your experience of Positive Nuclear IDentities, this law can be restated as:

The only motivation of all human behavior is to increase your experience of Positive Nuclear IDentities of Wisdom, Power, Value.

Every person works to be happy, FEEL good, and minimize activations of Negative Energy such as anger, sadness, fear, anxiety, depression, grief and all the other forms of Negative Emotion. Negative Emotion clouds thought which has a negative impact on your actions and behaviors, not only on the job but in all areas of your life.

Effective communication is critical to your success in both business and personal relationships. Unless you live in a cave your ability to successfully negotiate win-win in all areas of your life is your Power to create life as you would have it. Every action falls into the classification of DO or RELATE. These behaviors obey and can be understood in terms of the Causal Sequence. Following are some of the actual behaviors seen every day in an organization as a result of the Negative Nuclear IDentities. Most have to do with RELATE, an important component of DO.

Reflections *(also called Mirrors):*

Reflections are our interpersonal resistances, dislikes, and aversions. We dislike others because they trigger our dislikes for ourselves. The stronger the aversion we feel for the way another person is or acts, the stronger is the aversion for ourselves in whatever the other person triggers in us.

This is very easy to prove if you are sensitive to your internal energies, if you can feel your IDentities. Take any person that you dislike and write down exactly what you dislike in that person. Then turn off your mind, go into your experience, into pure feeling, and feel for something similar that you resist in you. It will always be there.

We resist and dislike others because they trigger our resistance and dislike of ourselves.

THERE IS NO OTHER REASON.

Take Response-ability or you will continue to live blaming others for how you are.

The IDentity triggered may not be exactly the same. For example, a thin person may dislike another person for being fat. But how can a thin person resist themselves for being fat? When we delve into the subconscious of the thin person, we find that the thin person has the mental equation that "fat is ugly". S/He is resisting the Nuclear Anti-Value IDentity of "I am ugly" triggered by the fat person.

Another example: A person who is meticulously clean may resist one who is sloppy or dirty. On delving inside, we find that the meticulously clean person has a compulsion to be clean as a response to their Nuclear Anti-Value IDentity of "I am dirty".

What you dislike in others is only a trigger for what you dislike in yourself.

Projection and Polarization:

Projection is a usually unconscious attempt to use Polarity to counter-act and to escape, the experience of Negative IDentities. It occurs when the negative expression of an IDentity quality, usually one of the Nuclear IDentities of Wisdom, Power, or Value, is projected onto others to reduce their BEingness of that quality. As the qualities are polarities, this makes it seem that we hold the high ground, the positive side of that quality. By making others less, we hope to be more.

One of the ways we project is with labels and epithets. By labeling others with such qualities as stupid, idiot, never do well, worthless, failure, etc., the labeler feels that he is, by comparison, superior in intelligence, ability, success, worthiness. This is always a projection of one's NIRs to the other to try to escape them, to appear more of that quality than others. If I make you the "bad" one, then I am the opposite polarity, the "good".

Polarization becomes involved in that it is understood that it is "bad" to be the negative polarity (ignorant, stupid, incapable, failure, weak, unworthy, undeserving, worthless). Creating the negative polarity as "bad" creates the illusion that one is justified in treating the other person with Negative Energy. This Negative Energy begins with the denial of SPace to BE as s/he is, and escalates through all the degrees of Negative Energy to attack, harm, and destroy.

Here are some common examples of Projection and Polarization at work:

You are stupid. <> I am intelligent.
You are the idiot. <> Therefore, I am smart.
You are bad. <> I am good.

You are incompetent. <> I can do it.

You are a failure. <> I am a success.

You are less than I (by whatever measure). <> I am better than you.

You are worthless. <> I am worthy.

You are wrong. <> I am right.

You don't deserve it. <> I am deserving.

Often, these communications are subtle, even done with a glance or a slight gesture. In the movie Titanic, the hero Jack was constantly subjected to inferences of ineptness, inferiority and unworthiness by the family of the heroine, Rose. This is also ego, explained in the next section. However, it is not by any means always subtle. If you will listen to people, especially when they are arguing, you will hear them use epithets quite clearly and directly. Projection plays a part in the following behaviors, which are themselves all related and often used together: Ego, Masks, Egoderas[25], Suppression.

Ego:

Ego is all efforts and behaviors that try to raise oneself up by putting others down; to create the illusion of being superior by making others inferior. Ego sees life as a teeter totter: I go up by putting you down. Ego is the intent to compensate one's Negative Nuclear IDentities by projecting them onto and in-validating others (make them less); thus trying to assume the "high ground" of the positive polarity to claim oneself as BE-ing more (more Knowledgeable, more Powerful, more Valuable), than others. All Ego is Projection and Polarization, but not all

---

25 Specific behaviors that are used to convince ourselves and others of our masks and superiority.

Projection is ego.

All Ego is an attempt to compensate NIRs:

Obviously, ego is a Negative Energy behavior. It will always provoke resistance, ego, and sabotage in others as they must defend their Nuclear Energy – it is the Imperative to do so.

Law: Ego Activates Ego.

For example, if a manager has a Negative IDentity of I AM WEAK, to not BE weak and therefore assume the opposite polarity, I AM POWERFUL the manager will make others appear weak.

In this way others are WEAK, and the manager, by comparison, is STRONG. Ego, then can be defined as all forms of intent to elevate BEing, not by "polishing" one's spirit, increasing personal excellence or achievement but by the invalidation of others. Ego is all efforts to increase the experience of Life energy of Wisdom, Power or Value, not by expressing more of these qualities but by trying to 'steal' them from others.

Consider Bill, a Supervisor of a team of 18. Bill doesn't get along with his boss and his last two reviews have been less than satisfactory. Below, see Ego at work in Bill's Causal Sequence of BE → FEEL → THINK → DO → HAVE:

BE: Bill in Negative IDentity of I AM incompetent, unable, ignorant, will attempt to compensate for these by assigning these undesirable qualities to his reporting people. In this way he appears to be the positive expression of these qualities. (At least in his mind)

FEEL: Bill feels Negative Emotional Energy: worthlessness, powerlessness, anger, fear, frustration, sadness, worry, desperation. The purpose of his behavior is to stop FEELing these Negative Emotions.

THINK: Bill will begin to calculate ways to aggrandize himself. He will be ambitious in the negative sense of the word. Extreme Ego is ruthless and can produce the Hitlers and Saddam Husseins of the world. Bill will use masks, mental creations of self to counter his Negative IDentities. For a Negative IDentity of I AM Less Than, Bill will create a mask of being better than others.

DO: Bill will begin to use specific behaviors to convince himself and others of his mask, his superiority. He may be pretentious, domineering, controlling, argumentative, or become a micro-manager. Bill may yell or be disrespectful to others to show strength and power. He will harass and threaten employees with termination in order to maintain control.

HAVE: As others resist Bill's Negative Energy, the result is reduced employee cooperation, sabotage, reduced initiative, low employee retention, retaliations and revenge, poor communications, absenteeism, avoidable mistakes – all of these leading to a team in chaos and reduced productivity.

All forms of Ego are intended to compensate for Negative Nuclear IDentities. Ego is an effort to Not BE a Negative IDentity. Instead of choosing to work on creating Positive IDentity within himself Bill has chosen instead to invalidate the BEing of others in order to elevate self. Ego is always Negative Energy toward others, the end result being resistance, whether overt (rebellion) or covert (sabotage). This resistance makes is difficult to achieve personal and organizational goals and objectives. Expressions of and words related to ego include: egoism, egotism, arrogance, bragging, lording, snobbism, flaunting, condescension, and pedantry.

Ego doesn't only show itself in the workplace. Ostentation to show one's power, wealth, or success is also a form of ego. In our society at large, many will pretend to be better than others as they show off ("ostentate") designer clothes and accessories. Much of the advertising industry lives by selling people expensive things they don't need so that they can try to compensate their Negative IDentities and BE-FEEL as smart, successful, and worthy as others. We even have names for it: "conspicuous consumption" and "keeping up with the Joneses".

Ego demands respect – that it has not earned—and so will often interpret others' behavior as impertinence or insolence. Ego always destroys good relations, cooperation, and support. Because of the Existential Imperative, people must seek to preserve and expand their nuclear energy. Therefore, they will resist ego which tries to reduce their sense of Wisdom, Power, and Value. They will resist openly if they can, and covertly through sabotage if they can't. Since Ego Activates Ego it is common that two people will get into an ego struggle, which often shows up as a power struggle.

The opposite of ego is humility, which we define as the accurate estimation of the value of oneself, leading to SPace and respect for all others. It can help us to overcome our ego to always remember, that in some way or another, every other person is always my superior. S/He always has past experiences, knowledge, and abilities that I do not.

For example, in Mexico in the mountains live people, the "indios", in families of 3 or 4 generations on small "ranchitos" (3 or 4, thatch-roof, mud-wall, dirt-floor huts in the middle of a couple of acres of land). They are very poor by American standards and most are illiterate. The few "rich" ones plow their fields with oxen. Most do so with a donkey or renting the oxen from the "rich". Nobody drives a car, much less has one, and the one dirt road back into the region is impassable whenever it rains. There is no electricity; water is carried from a spring 50 yards downhill. Yet these people need nothing of civilization: they live off the land as their ancestors have done for thousands of years. How many of us could do that except by learning from them? Were there some global catastrophe that should severely damage or destroy civilization they would hardly notice. They have the best job and financial security that exists.

What about you? Can you identify the egos of others against you? Can you see egos at large in your organization and the damage they do? But of most importance, can you identify your own ego at work? To improve your relationships and leadership abilities you need to retire it. The organization also needs to be conscious of ego in its leaders and eliminate it. Ego left unchecked in an organization will wreak havoc with the energy of the entire system. You are guaranteed a climate of resistance and sabotage.

Ego is eliminated by discreating the underlying, causal Negative Nuclear IDentities.

Masks: A mask is a pretense of BEing someone or some way that you are not. It is a fixed and ongoing psychological mechanism in which people pretend to be one way, to compensate how they really internally feel. Masks are attempts to compensate for Negative IDentities. Masks are commonly found with ego but may also exist without the invalidation of others. Masks are often accompanied by negative or obnoxious behaviors designed to convince self and others of the "truth" of the mask. Common masks and their compensation IDentities include:

- Strong (or Strong and Silent) <> I don't know; I am weak. I may say something stupid, better keep quiet.
- Know-it-all <> I don't know enough, I am ignorant, I am stupid.
- The Boss, "I give the orders around here" <> I am not sure how to succeed. I can fail.
- Super (man, woman, secretary, etc) <> I am afraid I won't be able to do it all; I could fail.

Mask-Ego behavior can show up as: Stuck up, presumptuous = I am better than you <> I am not good enough. (Remember the example of the movie Titanic above.)

Example: You will sometime see a woman who is physically dramatizing the concept of mask by putting on too much make-up and jewelry in an attempt to be attractive. This is a compensation for IDentities such as: "I am unattractive"; I am ugly".

It is necessary to distinguish between ego and mask and when a person truly has a quality, really is that way. This is easy; you just feel the energy. In other words, some women wear make-up just because they enjoy it. There may not be an IDentity of "I am unattractive." When there is ego, you will feel wary, uneasy, invalidated. When the person is truly competent in that way, you will feel at ease and natural. To see this, think back to your school days. You almost certainly had teachers who had lots of ego and teachers who had little; both were competent in the subject matter and good teachers.

Likewise, in your military or professional life you have had managers or supervisors who were full of ego and some who had little–they were genuinely smart, competent, wise). You can feel the difference, because as a spiritual being, you can naturally FEEL Negative Energy.

To see projection, polarization, ego, mask and suppression at work in the Causal Sequence take a look at the illustration below.

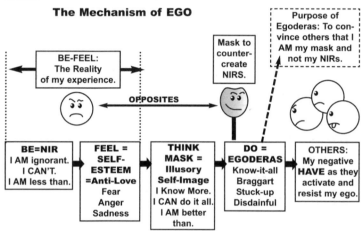

The Mechanism of EGO

The Causal Sequence in the previous diagram works like this:

1) The person is in NIRs (Negative Nuclear IDentities), and therefore FEELing unhappy, experiencing anger, fear, and/or sadness.

2) He creates a mental Mask of how he would like to BE. The Mask is always the polarity opposite of his NIRs. He usually ends up believing the Mask and so deluding himself.

3) The ego person then projects his NIRs = the negative polarity of his Mask to somebody else.

4) He then speaks and acts with egoderas (Negative DO such as arrogance, snobbery) to invalidate the qualities and abilities of others, to belittle or denigrate them.

5) His purpose is to drive them down in their apparent Power and Value, so that it appears that he is higher than, more Life Energy than they.

6) The Ego person sees life as a teeter-totter in which he goes up by putting others down. Of course, it does not work like this as others will always resist or sabotage ego.

Prejudice and Bigotry:

These are just another of the many forms of Projection, Polarization, Ego, and Masks. A person who is in a state of BEing inadequate, ignorant, stupid, incapable, less than others, will try to compensate for his NIRs by invalidating (make bad and wrong), polarizing, denying SPace, and treating others with Negative Energy. Intolerance is based in the delusional justification to invalidate another for inconsequential or uncontrollable characteristics.

Dictator:

A dictator uses overt Negative Energy to try to get others to obey his programs of how they should BE → THINK → DO →HAVE so that the dictator can assume a Positive BE-FEEL, in other words, be happy. Dictator differs from ego in that ego is not trying to change the other person, is not trying to get his cooperation or obedience. Ego only invalidates BE-FEEL to be superior. Dictator is trying to BE-FEEL good – move up out of a NIR to a PIR by getting what he wants of the other person(s). A dictator will always have programs of how others should BE, FEEL, THINK, DO, or HAVE. The Dictator will then exert Negative Energy pressure on the other person to comply with those programs. That pressure can take the form of anger attacks, accusations and invalidations, withdrawal of communication or support, threats, punishments, even physical abuse.

What the Dictator wants the other person to do is always against the other person's interests, desires, and happiness as that person perceives them. Thus, even though the Dictator often says that what he wants is in the best interest or for the happiness of the other person that is not true. The Dictator is seeking his own happiness and is perfectly willing for another to be unhappy in order to achieve it.

Many, many parents operate in Dictator with their children. They can get away with this as long as the children are too young to assert themselves. But once the children reach their teens and begin to flex their wings, they will rebel against the parental control and suppression of their BE → DO → HAVE. They will seek SPace (acceptance) with their peers, who often have a different set of values from the parents. If you see resistance and rebellion in children, you are looking at Dictator parents.

Likewise, the vast majority of problems between spouses are Dictator conflicts. One person wants the other to BE or DO in a certain way (programs). When the other fails to BE or DO so, the first person gets hurt or angry, and attacks or withdraws. Remember that all programs and all Negative Energy towards others always come out of NIRs and the External Quest. Again, the solution is discreation of NIRs to be in SPace to the BE DO HAVE of the other person. In the organization, almost everybody has their programs of how other people should BE and behave. Managers have their ideas of how employees should behave; subordinates have their ideas of how supervisors should behave. Behind the vast majority of anger in work relations, you will find frustrated Dictator. One person is angry because the other person would not BE or DO as that first person believed they should. The solution to this situation is discreation of NIRs to eliminate programs, and then communication to reach win-win agreements on behaviors.

Here are the questions to ask yourself to identify Dictators in your life are:

- Who in your life is trying to control you in any way and using some kind of Negative Energy to do so?
- Who in your life wants you to BE, FEEL, THINK, DO or HAVE in certain ways that you do not want to BE?
- Who in your life is treating you with Negative Energy because you do not fulfill their wants, needs, demands or expectations?
- Who in your life is treating you with Negative Energy because they are unhappy with who or how you are?

Then, of course, for true personal power you must ask yourself with whom are you being a Dictator. Determine for yourself the answer to the following questions:

- Who in your life is angry with you?
- Who is in resistance or rebellion to your input in their life?

Dictator is the denial of freedom and liberty to others to BE as they are, and to not-BE as they are not. It is the use of Negative Energy to invalidate and try to change and control others. You always resist the efforts of others to dictate and control you. You cannot expect them not to resist the Dictator in you.

In the workplace, it is necessary to distinguish between legitimate standards of behavior and performance, and personal programs about how other people should BE. This requires knowledge of what is being covered here and the ability to communicate well to understand another's viewpoints and programs. An effective leader will need to have continuous dialogue with his team to keep the energy clean and clear.

Victim:

The mechanism of Victim is very similar to that of Dictator. The difference is that the Victim does not feel that he has sufficient power to openly attack and control the other person. He tries to covertly manipulate with attacks of duty, obligation, blame and guilt.

The Victim often relies on programs implanted previously in the target person, often in childhood. These programs can include that the target person owes the Victim energy, obedience and respect because of all that the Victim has done and sacrificed for the target person, simply because the Victim is a relative. Victim is extremely common in families where parents, especially mothers, use it to manipulate their grown children.

In organizations, Victim operates a little differently. People will assume the position of Victim of a person in authority (their boss, for example), or of the organization itself, and use that to attract sympathy, pity, and support from others against that person or the organization. They may not have much real hope of effecting changes, but they get to make themselves right or superior. The Victim creates the organization as wrong and therefore justifies their sabotage. There is no real happiness in this, but it's the best that they can do with who they are and what they know.

Again we see the importance of the organization attacking the Cause Effect Polarity Scale and assisting its people in a move from the condition of Victim to Response-ability.

Suppression:

Suppression is an ongoing case of any of the above games and of any combination of them. Suppression is a continual effort to control others, to dictate as much as possible their BE and DO. The concept of a Godfather as portrayed in the movie of that name is an example of suppression. Many families are constituted around a suppressive patriarch or matriarch. And, of course, suppressive managers are common in business.

Suppressors want to control. The other side, the suppressee, lets himself be dominated because his program is that the suppressor should control (i.e. a parent). The suppressee believes he is dependent on the suppressor for approval and support. However beneath all suppression, and on both sides, suppressor and suppressee, there is always Negative Nuclear IDentities at work. A suppressor is a person in the negative polarity of Anti-Power and Anti-Value IDentities. He must try to compensate by wielding power over others. The suppressor remains a suppressee to avoid the activation of his negative Anti-Power and Anti-Value IDentities.

The solution to any and all of these mechanisms in human relationships is the discreation of the Negative Nuclear IDentities. Failing that, the solution is to understand Energy, the Existential Imperative, the Causal Sequence, the External Quest, the Cause-Effect Polarity, and SPace – all that you are now learning.

EVERY HUMAN BEHAVIOR OBEYS AND CAN BE UNDERSTOOD IN TERMS OF THE CAUSAL SEQUENCE.

All behavior is an attempt to control the Human Nuclear Energy; to escape negative BE-FEEL (Negative IDentities and Negative Emotions) and to achieve and maintain Positive IDentities and Emotions. When you truly understand this, you are an expert in the psychology of the human being.

Big BEings <> Little Beings:

At this point enough concepts have been presented to understand BEing more deeply. You now know that BEing is the polarity and quantity of the Nuclear Life Energy that consist of 4 "flavors": Wisdom, Power, Value, and Emotion. Each of these show up in life as different levels of BEing. Each of the qualities of BEing is a scale of many gradients from Little BEing to Big Being. However for simplicity, just the end point or conditions are described.

The Qualities of BEing

	WISDOM	CAUSE	SPACE	ENERGY
Big BEing Mostly operates in Positive Polarities.	Understands the Existential Imperative, Polarities, Cause-Effect, Victim-Responsability, the Causal Sequence, Identities, and how his BE FEEL THINK and happiness work. Can see the Causal Sequences of others easily and clearly.	Knows s/he is creator of their Quantum Energies, Emotions and Experience. Takes responsibility for their Negative Emotions and their relationships and so does not blame others for problems and conflicts thereby making themselves the victim. Is creative and proactive.	Does not create, and so lives free of, inter-pretations, stories, should not bes, and bads. Sees and deals with reality as it is. Does not Polarize others, giving people SPace to be as they are, and as they are not. Does not take things personally. Is mentally serene and thus able to THINK more clearly. Is free of masks and ego.	At Cause and operates only with Positive Energy. Continually discharges and dis-creates any negative energies. Is able to maintain serenity in the face of adverse events. Takes care to use positive energy with others. Never dumps activations on others.
Little BEing Mostly in Negative Polarities.	S/He is ignorant of how life works. Thinks their emotions are caused by external events and so wastes their life trying to control them. Lives neurotically trying to stop the "bad" behaviors of others, and to control the external world.	Denies responsibility for almost everything. Denies responsibility for their emotions and happiness. Believes that others can and should make them happy. Blames others for relationship problems and conflicts, and adverse events. Believes that they are the innocent victim of others and of life in general.	Mental Space is packed with negative creations. Does not see or deal with reali-ty, but with personal interpretations, distor-tions, judgments, par-adigms, and pro-grams. Has a big ego, strong masks. Full of preju-dices and bigotry. Sees everything as polarized for or against them, as good or bad, right or wrong. Takes many things personally. Polarizes others.	Generates lots of negative energy. Responds negatively to the negative energy of others. Is frequently activated in negative nuclear identities and there-fore in negative emotions such as anger, anxiety, fear, loneliness, grief, and depression. When activated, dumps his negative energy on the people around him.

Qualities and Actions of a Powerful BEing:

* Mostly operates in Positive Polarities. Understands the Existential Imperative, Polarities, Cause-Effect, Victim-Responsability, the Causal Sequence, IDen-tities, and how BE FEEL THINK and happiness work. S/He can see the Causal Sequences of others easily and clearly; S/He knows S/He is creator of her/

his Quantum Energies, Emotions and experience.

- S/He takes responsability for Negative Emotions and their relationships and so does not blame others for problems and conflicts thereby creating Victim.
- Is creative and proactive: Does not create distortions and illusions, and so lives free of, interpretations, stories, should not's and bads. S/He sees and deals with reality as it is.
- S/He does not Polarize others, giving people SPace to be as they are, and as they are not.
- S/He does not take things personally. S/He is mentally serene and thus able to THINK more clearly.
- S/He is free of masks and ego; lives at Cause and operates only with Positive Energy.
- S/He continually discharges and discreates any Negative Energies. S/He is able to maintain serenity in the face of adverse events. S/He takes care to use Positive Energy with others.
- S/He never dumps her activations on others.

Quality and Actions of a Diminished BEing:

- Mostly in Negative Polarities.
- Is ignorant of how life works.
- S/He believes emotions are caused by external events and so wastes his/her life trying to control them.
- S/He lives neurotically trying to stop the "bad" behaviors of others, and to control the external world.
- S/he denies responsability for almost everything

and denies responsability for his/her own emotions and happiness.

- S/He believes that others can and should make them happy. S/He blames others for relationship problems and conflicts and adverse events.
- S/He believes that they are the innocent victim of others and of life in general. Mental Space is packed with negative creations. S/He does not see or deal with reality, but with interpretations, distortions, judgments, paradigms, and programs.
- S/He has a big ego and strong masks, often full of prejudices and bigotry. Often S/He sees everything as polarized for or against him/her and as good or bad, right or wrong.
- S/He takes many things personally.
- S/He polarizes others; S/He generates much Negative Energy and responds negatively to the Negative Energy of others.
- S/He is frequently activated in Negative Nuclear IDentities and therefore in Negative Emotions such as anger, anxiety, fear, loneliness, grief, and depression. When activated, s/he dumps their Negative Energy on others.

People are the basic chip, the basic generator of energy and therefore power in the organization. Everybody in the organization is somewhere on the scale of BEing that you see above. Their ability to avoid the generation of Negative Energy and to produce Positive Energy is a function of their level of BEing, and that is a function of the Nuclear Energy of BEing: Wisdom,

Power, Value, SPace and Emotion.

Now we can expand our original law, the Existential Imperative, that "The Ultimate Motivation of all human behavior is happiness"—to a more expanded statement: "The Ultimate Motivation of all human behavior is more Life, more BEing, to BE and therefore FEEL more of the life energies of Wisdom, Power, Value, and Happiness. The Ultimate Motivation of all human effort and behavior is to experience more and more positive spiritual Nuclear Energy.

This expansion of your BEing, of the spiritual Life Energy that you are, is in fact, the purpose of existence. The center of Life, is not the work that you do in the physical universe; it is the work that you do on your Self. If you do not have your Self as the center of your life, you will be going around in circles and not getting much of anywhere.

Notice that the infinity of the Nuclear Life Energies is INFINITE LIFE, the INFINITE ENERGY: CONSCIOUSNESS, WISDOM, CAUSE POWER, HAPPINES & JOY.

On one hand, we have the fact that more BEing, ever more Nuclear Life Energy is the motivation and the purpose of existence.

On the other, we have the fact that the performance of your employees, and therefore of your organization, is in direct proportion to the amount of BEing (Wisdom, Power, Value, and therefore Positive Emotion) that they are expressing.

Therefore, the ultimate purpose of an organization should be to increase the BEing, the Nuclear Energies of all employees. This is both what is best for your teams, what they most want and seek, what motivates them; and it is best for the survival and flourishing of the organization: to have employees operating in optimal Life Energy, Positive BEing, Responsability and Personal Power.

Life is fundamentally Quantum, about non-physical energy, about spirit. Whenever you put materiality before spirit, you will experience a loss of both Power and Happiness, and an increase in Negative Energy, problems, and conflicts.

But Energies rarely work alone. To be powerful, to produce many and great results, many forms of energy must align and cooperate in Energy Systems. Every individual is an energy system; a family is an energy system; a group or department is an energy system; a factory is an energy system; every business or organization is an energy system; a nation is an energy system; as is the entire planet. Energy works in synergy, which is the synchronization of energies so that the power of the whole system is far beyond that of any element; the system lacking even one element cannot operate successfully.

The Human Energy Climate of an organization is the net combination of all the human mental, emotional, and behavioral energies, both positive and negative. Positive Human Energy, which includes commitment, intelligence, initiative, creativity and good relationships with others, is the basis of a smooth operation and determines the production results of the organization. Negative Human Energy expressed as Negative Emotion such as hostility, anxiety or sadness, is what causes interpersonal frictions, problems, and errors that interfere with operations and therefore with production in both quality and quantity. The Energy Climate can be felt as the overall morale, motivation, enthusiasm and individual fulfillment in the organization. The success and power of your organization depends on its energy, your understanding of Energy Systems and the effective handling of

Quantum Energy.

Production and money are not the prime purpose of any Group Energy System or business. Not only are they secondary purposes, but they are by-products of how well you fulfill the primary purpose of increasing the Quantum Nuclear Energy of the people in your organizations, families and communities.

Many people have money and material things such as success and power as their highest goals only because they do not understand the nature of Life, the nature of themselves as non-physical, spiritual beings. Until now, neither you are those around you understood the nature of happiness. As a result of this ignorance, they seek happiness where it does not exist by means that are impossible to be successful, by means of the External Quest, the search for Happiness outside of oneself.

As organizations center themselves around these principles you will see a quantum leap in motivation and energy of your workforces that will result in notable increases in the quantity and quality of the organizational results.

In the global market and information sphere of today, competitive advantages from purely physical advances are fleeting. Information, technologies, and products travel too fast. The next frontier of competition is not physical science and technology; it will be the harnessing of human Quantum Energy and science. The next challenge of business is Human Nuclear Energy development – to Power the organization. The organization that understands and operates to unleash the Human Nuclear Energy is the wave of the future.

CONCLUSION

The Next Step — Where do you go from here?

How to Create Responsability in Your Organization:

- Teach others by your example
- Look for opportunities to empower others
- Share the knowledge that you have gained in this book
- Attend a LEAD Seminar (See page 218 for details)

While all of the above can be significant to your success the most powerful action you can take is to carefully examine YOU. Acknowledge your own Negative Quantum Energies and resolve to no longer resist them, but to work through them. In this way you will increase your own personal Power and move towards a life of happiness and serenity.

Begin with the knowledge that if you are to achieve success you must first establish a vision. Without a vision neither you, your family, your business, your community or any organization of which you are a part, will have any idea of which direction to take. A clear vision provides clarity on where you are to go. Visions allow you to map out your course with the details of how to get there. Visions identify goals and objectives, allow you to create a map, estimate distance, time and effort and tell you when you are deviating from the optimum course. Visions allow you to identify possible blocks and obstacles. In the same way that organizations create visions, you must also establish a vision for YOU. And as parent, leader, manager, spouse, friend, co-worker— you can encourage others to do the same. Everyone is navigating life; those with a vision know where they are going. Without a vision you cannot establish priorities, recognize what is important, people that can help you, find the resources that are available to you, focus your time and energy so you know how to live on purpose. Without a vision you are floating through life as driftwood along the sea.

Visions are mental images of something that you wish to create or manifest or achieve. Organizations have visions, just as each member of the organization should as well. A business plan is a physical recording of a mental vision, that which is to be created. The archer must have a target, the artist starts with a sketch, the architect begins with a blueprint. You create your Life twice; first in the Quantum Universe and then in the physical universe. The first is the vision, a vision of that which is to be created. There are no accidents, coincidences, randomness in life. Despite appearances, nothing happens by accident. Organizations and people are creative. Just as you create everything in your experience, organizations create their experience as well, positive and negative.

Your creative power in life comes from understanding the importance of your vision of what you wish to create. To manifest a vision all you have to do is energize it. Your attention, your Energy, whether it be positive or negative, creates and attracts. When you or the organization is in Negative Emotion you are energizing and therefore creating and attracting what you don't want. This is how the creative process works. How much time do people in your organization spend in sabotage, resentment, rebellion, discontent, negative attitude or frustration?

Consider your own life – what percentage of your time and energy is in anxiety, sadness, guilt, resentment, anger, fear, grief, apathy, depression or any negative emotion? Energy is creative regardless of its positive or negative polarity. When you don't understand how the creation process works you will create less of what you do want and a lot more of what you don't want. This is not because of an innate lack of power but ignorance of how the creative process works, both in organizations and in your own life. In order to achieve Power in Life you must understand how to control your Emotions, how to control Energy, how to control the contents of your mind. When you live the life that you want, you will live in enthusiasm, desire, passion and joy.

This is the outcome of a worthy vision. Your visions have power. They have the power to motivate and move you to action, they have the power to direct the universe to move into your life the events, people and resources you need to manifest your visions. The universe is alive and responds to the passion of your visions. Your visions are your communications to the universe of what you and your organization will create. Your vision is to the universe a communication of what to manifest around you. Now stop and consider this—do you have a clear vision of where your team is going? Does each member of your team have a clear vision and is it the same vision? Do you have a clear vision of your organization? Of far more significance, what about you? Where are you going in Life? Do you have a clear precise, specific vision for your life?

To assist you in your journey please take advantage of the accompanying free workbook: *The Science of Leadership: A Workbook of Self-Discovery.* In This workbook you will find exercises to guide you in charting a clear Vision, navigating your current Causal Sequences and creating those that you wish to experience. To download this free workbook visit:

www.GalileoConsultants/visionworkbook.html

More on The LEAD Program:

The LEAD Program is a curriculum of training courses for all levels of employees. Currently available are two seminars:

LEAD for Leaders, Managers and Supervisors
LEAD for Associates

These seminars further expand on the information provided in this book. The premise of these seminars is that people are the ultimate source of energy and therefore the Power of an organization. An organization is a complex Energy System. Positive Human Quantum Energy is the POWER that gets things done and produces the goals of the organization. Negative Human Quantum Energy is the primary cause of conflicts, problems, decrease in production and therefore profitability of an organization. It is this Negative Human Quantum Energy that reduces the power of an organization much more so than problems with equipment, budget constraints or other physical systems of the organization. The Human Quantum Energy System includes the mind, the emotions, motivations, communications, behaviors and relationships operating within people. Failure to understand how the Human Quantum Energy System works ensures decreased results.

These seminars will teach you how to transform the Energy Climate of your organization. These seminars are not motivational or inspirational as neither of these last for long. These seminars are designed to create permanent changes in the way people think, feel, treat and react to each other. In order to achieve optimal results you must understand that your organization is a powerful complex Energy System. Power is the ability to produce high quality and sufficient quantity of products and services that please customers and therefore generate income and profits. Positive Power is the Energy that gets things done and achieves the results that you desire. For information on seminars for your business contact:

Victoria DePaul
Email: Info@GalileoConsultants.com
Telephone: 508-770-0550
Website: www.GalileoConsultants.com

GLOSSARY

Accountability: The "response" part of Responsability in which a person is responded to and responds for his actions. Accountability is that characteristic of an Energy System which justly rewards Positive Energy contributions and requires payment of Consequences for Negative Energy and losses. Accountability is part of Justice and Fairness.

Activation: The stimulation or triggering of an NIR Mass, which consists of a Negative Nuclear IDentity, a creation of "It's bad to BE that way", and a charge of Negative Energy that is experienced as unpleasant emotion. An activation is primarily felt as a mass or charge of Negative Emotions. Activations are the only source of UPS that exist.

Bad: That which "should not be", thereby seeming to justify the use of Negative Energy to stop, change, punish or destroy it. It must be noted that emotional energy is the only UPS that exists, and that the first person to suffer Negative Energy is always the person who attacks the "bad". We must distinguish between things that are really bad because they do indeed cause unjustified pain, damage, or destruction; and those that are created "bad" by the mind. Most "bad" things fall into this classification of mind illusions. Particularly, it must be noted that a trigger is not bad just because a person activates when it occurs; the trigger is not the cause of the emotional pain, but rather the person's failure to control his Nuclear IDentities. Therefore, triggers, unless they are actually generating Negative Energy are not bad.

BE: The first element of the Causal Sequence. The state, conditions, or modulation of the Energy that gives any particular form or mass of energy its individuality, qualities, and characteristics –its IDentity, its uniqueness—and therefore its distinction from all other forms of Energy. In a human being, the primary BEingness is the polarity and degree of BEing (and therefore FEELing oneself as) the Nuclear Energies of Wisdom, Power, Value, and Emotion. There are many forms of secondary states of BE (IDentities), including the roles such as father, mother, businessmen, teacher, etc. These secondary identities are not covered in this book.

BEing: An individualization of the ONE LIFE ENERGY of Consciousness, Cause, Will, Value, Love, Joy (WPVLJ). The individualized spirit which is the human being, the Aware Will / Conscious Cause, that resides in and controls the body to play in the physical universe. The basic BEing made of the Nuclear Energies then determines what more s/he is or is not being through the creation of IDentities.

Bigotry: The attempt to escape an inferiority complex (NIRs) by projecting and polarizing others to the inferior position so that self can seem to assume the superior polarity. Bigotry is impersonal ego en masse to an entire group or class of persons.

Blame: To make bad and wrong for failed Cause

Cause: The "north" end of the Cause-Effect Polarity. **Verb:** The action and process of bringing into being or changing something. The action of originating, starting, creating, controlling, changing, moving, producing, affecting, or effecting something. The action of producing an effect. **Noun:** The agent of force and action that effects change. That which originates, initiates, creates, manifests, decides, determines, acts, forms, produces, gives, moves, controls, changes, or affects anything. The concept of Cause includes: Will, Power, Force, Creator, Creation, and Production.

Causal Sequence: The formula of How Life Works: BE→FEEL → THINK → RELATE / DO → HAVE (abbreviated BFTRDH). The Causal Sequence can also be expressed as: IDENTITY → EMOTION → MIND → SPEAK / ACTIONS → RESULTS where each element in the second statement of the sequence is equivalent to the corresponding element in the first statement. The Causal Sequence says: Who I AM (BE) determines What I FEEL which determines How I THINK which determines my SAYings and DOings which are how I communicate & treat others, and How I ACT and behave. My ACTIONS determine my Results=HAVE in life. Your life consists of your Causal Sequences. Everything in your life falls into one of these five areas. It is life itself. It is a Causal Sequence because each element determines the following ones. The beauty of the Causal Sequence is that you only need to learn to control the first element, your BEing, to control all the rest of your life. Your life functions according to the Causal Sequence whether you know it or not, and whether you want it to or not. There is no escaping it: it controls your existence.

Consequence(s): Natural or agreed-upon energy output to repair or restore the results of negative action.

Create: To Cause something to exist within your experience for the first time.

Discreate: To Cause something to no longer exist by releasing its energy modulation and form back into free energy.

Dictator: The extremely common mechanism in relationships where one person tries to dictate to another how BE, FEEL, DO, etc., i.e. according to the Dictator's programs. The purpose of the dictation (programs) is to control the Dictator's BE-FEEL. When the person complies, the Dictator assumes a Positive BE-FEEL. When the person does not comply, the Dictator remains in or activates even more negative BE-FEEL and usually dumps Negative Energy (anger, blame, withdrawal, etc) on the non-complying person. Most relationship conflicts, especially in families, are Dictator problems.

DO: The fourth element of the Causal Sequence. All actions, behaviors, and efforts. DO has two divisions: Actions with material things; and RELATE; communication and dealings with others.

Ectropy: The Intelligent Casual Force of Life that distinguishes, orders, and synergizes energy and matter into Energy Systems, thus to have ever more Power. The force and power of Life to be Intelligent Cause: to create, change, move, order, heat, and organize. As opposed to Entropy which is the tendency of matter-energy existing without Life Force control to chaos, cold, and stillness.

Effect: The "south" pole of the Cause-Effect polarity. **Verb**: and to cause something, to create an effect, to produce an effect, to carry out an action to a successful result. **Noun:** 1- The influence, change, affect or result produced by a Cause. Examples: The effect of a bomb is destruction. The effect of a Quantum reality on consciousness is experience. Synonyms: result, impact, outcome.

The condition of Effect in people, is a condition of no power, no control; of living affected or controlled by an external cause. This is also known as the condition of Victim. However, Effect / Victim in people is always an illusion: BEings are ALWAYS Cause.

Ego: All efforts to invalidate, suppress or "steal" Nuclear Energy from others so that one appears to BE more, and therefore superior in BEing (Knowledge, Power, Value, Love-ability) to others. The Polarization of others (usually in the areas of the Nuclear Energies), so that one can seem to be better and more deserving than others. Ego is always Negative Energy and will be resisted by others

Emotions, Emotional Energy Polarity: Emotions are energies. Joy, passion, love, enthusiasm, satisfaction, monotony, indifference, anger, fear, anxiety, rage, worry, guilt, resentment, hate, sorrow, loneliness, sadness, grief, desperation, depression, etc. – all of these are energies. As is all experience, emotions are a polarity.

ENERGY, The ENERGY; When spelled with all capitals, it refers to THE ONE INFINITE, INTELLIGENT CAUSAL LIFE FORCE which is both CREATOR and created, and the ESSENCE of all that exists. The Nucleus of the ENERGY is the qualities of Wisdom, Power and Value, which also the Essence or Nuclear Energies of the human spirit.

Energy: Everything that exists is made of and moved by Energy, of which there are an infinity of kinds and forms, frequencies and modulations. Energy is the basic substance of the cosmos. Even solid matter is energy, as shown by Einstein's famous formula, $E=mc2$, and demonstrated by the existence of stars, nuclear power plants, and atom bombs.

Energy Climate: The overall sense or feeling of energy in a person or an **Energy System:** It is a polarity ranging from very negative (depressed, pessimistic, at Effect, no power, can't do, going to fail; etc to very positive (at Cause, can do, enthusiasm, passion, confidence.) It is basically the condition of the Nuclear Energy in the system.

Energy System: Any group of two or more energies or entities that cooperate to produce results (Power) greater than either could alone. Energy systems are synergy: synchronized energy. External or Group Energy Systems run from coupleships to the entire planet, and even the entire universe. Each human being is internally also an energy system.

Entropy: That characteristic of Matter, as the opposite polarity of Life, to decay and deteriorate to the lowest possible energy state and to maximum dispersion and homogeneity of materials. The tendency of matter-energy left unattended by Life to disorganization, chaos, cold and stillness. The death force. The opposite of Ectropy.

Essence: Synonym for the Life / BEing / Nuclear Energies of Wisdom, Power, Value. The Essence or Nucleus of BEing is the WPV energy. "ESSENCE" in all capitals is a synonym for the INFINITE LIFE FORCE: see LIFE.

Event, External Events: Any change or movement that you perceive around you. It can be anything that anybody says or does, any occurrence, any perception of a situation or circumstance. It can be the arrival or departure of a person or thing, or your own arrival or departure from a situation or place. The word is used most generally to mean any change or movement.

Existential Imperative, Experiential Imperative: The supreme command and compulsion within every human being to avoid or escape the BE-FEEL / experience of Negative Nuclear Energy (NIR Masses), and to move "upward" into ever higher levels of Positive Nuclear Energy = Life Essence = Wisdom, Power, Self-Esteem and Happiness. You have no choice in the matter; you must obey the Existential Imperative. It manifests as the External Quest when a person does not know how life works.

Experience: General term for all perception and "savoring" of anything, physical or Quantum. Each element of the Causal Sequence (BE-FEEL → THINK → DO → HAVE) is one kind of experience, and the experiences possible within each kind are infinite. BE is experience of Self; FEEL is emotional experience: THINK is all experience in the mind, all forms of thought and thought processes. DO is all action and relationship experience; and HAVE is the experience of all material things and situations. Most forms of experience are Polarities and all the Laws of Polarity apply. To Control Experience is the ONLY motivation of all human behavior.

External Quest: The impossible effort of trying to control the external world to create internal happiness. Trying to control (DO) the External World (HAVE) to stop or destroy triggers (to avoid activations); and to find, get, and hoard whatever material thing or circumstance one THINKS will bring happiness. The External Quest is trying to live life backwards: THINK DO HAVE to try to control BE-FEEL (happiness). This is impossible. See also Fatal Paradigm, the THINK that setups up the External Quest. See also the opposite, The Internal Quest.

Fatal IDentity: The BEing is Cause, Creator, Powerful. The BEing, however, as Creator, can counter-create his Cause by declaring and so creating, the IDentity that s/he is not Cause. This does not stop the BEing from being Cause, but creates the illusion and experience of not being Cause. This, blinds the person to awareness of his Cause-Power, and creates the illusion and experience of being Effect, aka Victim.

The Fatal IDentity is any variant of: I am not Cause: I am Not Creator. I am Not Responsable. I am not Powerful, I am a Victim. They are called the Fatal IDentity because they "kill" the person's awareness of his Power, and send the person into the Anti-Power Nuclear IDentities with their attendant Negative Emotion to Self of frustration, anger, fear, sorrow, and depression. Thus, the Fatal IDentity "kills" the person's Power, ability to experience happiness. Underneath the illusion of the Fatal IDentity, the person continues to create his life, but the process is blocked from his perception and therefore beyond his control. Events appear to be random and happening without the person's input – which is the condition of Victim. See the Cause-Effect, Victim-

Responsability Polarity for more information.

Fatal Paradigm: The negative THINK that is the natural result of the Fatal IDentity. The Fatal Paradigm is the belief that (as I am Not Cause, the Fatal IDentity); external events cause my experience /emotions. I am Effect: they are Cause. The Fatal Paradigm has two sides: 1) External events cause my pain and suffering (therefore, I must attach and change them). 2) External events will eventually make me happy (if only I can find the right thing and hoard enough of it). Both send the person on the Impossible External Quest of trying to control the world to be happy: THINK→DO→HAVE to try to control BE-FEEL.

FEEL: The second element of the Causal Sequence. FEEL is all emotional experience. All FEELing is experience; not all experience is FEELing; there is also self, mental, and physical experience. FEEL consists of the Emotional Energy Polarity that is the Positive Emotion <> Negative Emotion Polarity that is the Happiness <> UPS Polarity.

GIGO: An old computer term standing for, "Garbage In, Garbage Out". It means that whenever there are flaws or errors in the programming, the computer cannot produce the desired results. In other words, in an energy system, problems with DO and HAVE are often in the THINK.

Guilting: Trying to instill guilt in another person for something they did or failed to do. This is done by convincing the other person that what s/he did was bad, and therefore s/he is bad for having done it, which activates the only source of guilt in life: the Nuclear Anti-Value IDentity, "I am bad".

Happiness: A state of Positive Nuclear Energy (Wisdom, Power, Value), and especially of fourth Nuclear Energy, Positive Emotional Energy, almost all the time, no matter and unfazed by external events and situations.

HAVE: The fourth element of the Causal Sequence. All the material things, events, situations, circumstances, and people that appear in a person's life. Includes money and financial condition. NOT HAVE is all the things that a person wants and has not been able to produce. NEGATIVE HAVE is all the things that a person has that the person does not want, but has not been able to eliminate from his life.

Histories: See Stories

HOS: see Human Operating System

Human Nuclear Energy: see Nuclear Energy, Human.

Human Operating System (HOS): The collection of paradigms, ideas, and beliefs (THINK), mostly unconscious, with which
a person is operating his Causal Sequences of FEEL, DO, and HAVE
(metaphysical energies, emotions, relationships, and physical life). Errors in the HOS are GIGO and lead to the generation of Negative
Energy, pain and suffering, relationship problems and conflicts, and
general inability to produce the desired results in life. As Life works
THINK→DO→HAVE, for a person to improve their life, they must
correct the flaws in their HOS.

Identity: Any creation / declaration by Self of what or who one is
or is not. Identities usually take the form of statements of I AM or I
AM NOT. Most are polarities. The Nuclear IDentities are the declaration of Self in the areas of Wisdom, Power, and Value. See also PIRs
and NIRs.

Positive Nuclear IDentities (PIRs)

WISDOM

POWER

VALUE

I Am Intelligent.

I Am Creative.

I Know.

I Am Smart.

I Learn quickly and easily.

I Am Capable.

I Can Do It.

I Am Strong.

I Am A Success.

I Am Powerful.

I Am Worthy.

I Deserve.

I Am Good Enough.

I Am Important.

I Am Valuable.

Negative Nuclear IDentities (NIRs)

ANTI-WISDOM

ANTI-POWER

ANTI-VALUE

I Am Ignorant.

I Am Dumb.

I Am Stupid.

I Can't Learn.

Studying Is Hard.

I Can't; I Am Unable.

I Am Incapable.

I Am Weak.

I Am Useless.

I Am A Failure.

I Am Not Worthy.

I Don't Deserve.

I Am Less Than Others.

I Am Not Good Enough.

Nobody Loves Me.

Internal Quest: All efforts to restore one's Life Essence, the Nuclear Energies of WPV, and therefore Happiness, by working on one's BE-ing (Self) directly (with creation and discreation). The Internal Quest has two sides: 1) Discreate the NIR Masses that suppress our experience of our natural Essence. 2) Create and affirm PIRs, the Nuclear IDentities. Discreation of the NIR Masses should be balanced 30—70 with creating and affirming the Nuclear Energies. The Internal Quest is the polar opposite of the External Quest, and is the ONLY way to find true love, joy and happiness in life.

Interpretations and Meanings: The mental creation and assignment of meanings and significance to events. These are always distortions of the Facts, the objective Truth of what happened. People then react and trigger on, not Reality, but to their interpretations of Reality. The fundamental Law is "Nothing means anything until you create it so." Life is a parade of events. Each person creates what any event means. The wise man does not create meanings for events.

LIFE: When spelled with all capitals, it refers to THE ONE INFINITE, INTELLIGENT CAUSAL LIFE FORCE which is both CREATOR and created, and the Essence of that exists. The Essential Characteristics of LIFE are the energies of Wisdom, Power, and Value which are also the Essence or Nuclear Energies of the human spirit. When spelled with a capital L only, the word refers to the process of Life, of birth, growth, change, and decay on this planet. When spelled "life", it refers to the life of an individual.

Mind: See THINK. Mind is purely thoughts and the thought processes and manipulations.

MOD: Moment of Dolor (Latin for Pain). Synonym for the activation of Negative Emotion and its causal NIR. The triggering into experience of a NIR Mass. As most people resist their MODs, these tend to persist much longer than the polarity opposite MOPs.

MOP: Moment of Pleasure. The temporary, fleeting, externally-triggered activation of a PIR Mass (I won; I could do it, I am loved, etc. plus the corresponding Positive Emotional Energy charge) when the person achieves some goal or positive surprise. As there is no real control by the person of his IDentities, these soon pass—often replaced by a MOD. MOPs are dangerous in that they create the mirage that happiness is caused by external things and thus reinforce the External Quest.

Negative: That which is unpleasant, undesired, or counter-productive to one's goals. Not to be confused with "bad". Negatives are not bad (implying should not be and change or destruction). Negatives must exist for the positive to exist, and may later be a positive if ones values or goals change.

Negative IDentity Realities, see NIRs.

Negative Nuclear IDentities: see NIRs

NIRs: Negative IDentity Realities, synonym for Negative Nuclear IDentities. Any creation of Self as Anti-Wisdom, Anti-Power or Anti-Value IDentities, which will then trigger Negative Emotion. Your Negative Emotion to Self is the ONLY UPS that exist. The opposite polarity is PIRs. For examples of both, see IDentity.

NIR Mass: One or more NIRs with its creation of "bad to be that NIR", plus the corresponding charge of Negative Emotion to self. By discreating first the bad, the Negative Emotion disappears and the path is clear to integrate with and discreate the NIR.

Nucleus, adj. Nuclear: That which is at the very center of anything. That which is the most basic essence of anything, most central to its nature and identity.

Nuclear Energy, Human: The most powerful energy in the cosmos is the LIFE ENERGY FORCE that is FIRST CAUSE and CREATOR of all else. It is the ENERGY from which everything that exists is made, and which moves all that moves, and which animates life forms. We abbreviate the many characteristics of this ENERGY to four component energies called: Wisdom, Power, Value, and Emotion. We denominate these four energies the Nuclear Energies of BEing, of spirit, as they are the fundamental and centric forces of the human spirit, and of the INFINITE LIFE ENERGY: The human spirit is formed of this energy; it is an individualization of this NUCLEAR LIFE ENERGY.

Persistence: The continued existence of something over time, especially important when that something is negative and we wish to be free of it.

Personalization: To take personally and create offense and activation about the actions of another person. Personalization is usually an interpretation as the creation and assignment of a (bad) intention on the part of another person to insult or offend where it did not exist. The root cause of personalization is always one's NIRs.

PIRs: Positive IDentity Realities, synonym for Positive Nuclear IDentities: Any creation or affirmation of Self as Wisdom, Power, or Value IDentities, which will then trigger the Positive Emotions of Self. PIRs Self-Love is the only Happiness that exists. The opposite polarity is NIRs. For examples of both, see IDentity.

Polarity: The stretching of a concept into two opposing directions (towards two poles), thereby creating a range of degrees, a spectrum of possibilities, of that energy / experience.

Polarization: The division and separation of people or groups

231

based on distortions of Anti-Value (good <> bad, right <> wrong, superior<> inferior, worthy<>unworthy, etc.), so that the "bad" group is excluded from equal rights and participation, and may be attacked, harmed, or even killed.

Power: The ability to produce the desired results. The ability to do work, towards producing a desired result. Does not mean force, or domination. True Power is power with, not power over.

Programs: Any mental requirement of how something, especially other people, should or should not BE-FEEL, THINK, DO, or HAVE. One of the many forms of distortions and delusions of the mind about Reality and Life and other BEings. The purpose of a program is to dictate how externals should be in order to control one's BE-FEEL (IDentities and Emotions). Therefore, most people trigger when others do not comply with their programs, thereby causing themselves pain and usually attacking the non-complying person. Programs are involved in the grand majority of relationship conflicts (as are NIRs which they are intended to control). Programs are one form of Should / Should Not BE – see this for more information.

Quantum Energy: Quantum Energies are those which can not be produced or measured by physical means or equipment, but are generated by LIFE itself. They include the Human Nuclear Energies of Wisdom, Power and Value. These include will, consciousness, mind, all thoughts and mental process, information: all the emotions, love, happiness, the impulses and compulsions to behaviors, for example, addictions, and all relationships. Bodies are physical, but communication and relationships are Quantum.

Punishment: Loss, pain or suffering caused to retaliate for a negative action or result, sometimes in the hope that fear of future punishment will restrain that action.

Reality: With a capital R means the external Reality of the world as it is at any moment. It is synonym for What Is, As It Is.

RELATE: The first part of the fourth element of the Causal Sequence, DO. What you SAY and DO, how you communicate and behave in your dealings with others.

Resistance: First Level: the refusal to BE, FEEL, or otherwise experience something. Second Level: The generation of Negative Energy to avoid, stop, change, harm, punish, or destroy something.

Resistance Causes Persistence: (Law). The feeding of energy, even though Negative Energy, into anything actually energizes that thing and makes it stronger and more persistent.

Responsability, Response-ability: The midpoint of transition between Effect and Cause on the Cause-Effect Spectrum. Response-ability is the ability to respond. To respond to or for something is to take action (DO) in some way to handle that thing or situation. Responsability, then, is the ability to act. To act is to be in a condition of CAUSE. Any condition of possibility of action, including when experiencing negative effects caused by others. If you can act to avoid or remedy something, you are response-able. Consciousness of Cause; acknowledgement and awareness of being Cause, of being able to act. The ability to respond deliberately under self-control and reason; as opposed to out-of-control emotional reaction. Logical choice and control, as opposed to emotional reactivity and resistance. The ability to vary your actions and responses until you achieve the desired result (as opposed to repeating over and over an ingrained habit or behavioral rut). The duty or privilege to care for someone or something, which is to be at Cause for its well-being. Accountability (Justice): The ability and the duty to respond for our negative actions, to restore damaged or lost energy. Without Accountability, Responsability does not exist – nor does Justice. A counterpart of Freedom. Freedom can only exist where there is Responsability (and Accountability) for the results of using that freedom.

Sabotage: The condition of a person contributing less than his best, less than 100% of his energy, to any system to which he has declared or owes loyalty.

Should / Should Not BE: (S/SNB) One of the many forms of distortions and delusions of the mind about What Is. Once something Is, one's opinions (mental creations) as to whether it should or should not be, are irrelevant and a waste of time and energy. The real question is: What do we want and do now? S/SNB is deadly to happiness as people let themselves trigger on and resist events because they THINK those events should not be. Thus, people trigger on their hallucinations, not on Reality. See also Programs.

SPace: No-thing-ness. It is the absence of all energy (includes matter). Pure Awareness without thought or emotion. Mentally, SPace is the absence of thoughts and of interpretations, personalizations, should not be, programs, "bads". Thus, SPace is the condition of the perception of Reality and Truth free of mental distortions. Mental SPace creates emotional SPace, the absence of emotion, but especially of the Negative Emotions that are pain and suffering. SPace is the absence of activations, and is therefore, peace and serenity. SPace for Self and for others is the absence of opinions and programs and therefore of resistance, so that it is liberty to BE as one is, and let others BE as they are. Thus, SPace as the end of Dictator programs, should not be, bads, and Negative Energy resistance, is the beginning of love and good relationships. SPace is the midpoint, the transition point on many Polarity Spectrums between the positive and negative polarities. These spectrums include Cause <> Effect, Happiness <> UPS; Value+/- ; Good <> Bad; and the Emotional Energy Spectrum. SPace is the effective way to control Negative Energy, as Negative Energy (resistance) against Negative Energy only piles up Negative Energy and creates persistence.

Spectrum: A range or scale of degrees of possibilities of experience between two poles. See Polarity.

Stories and Histories: Long, involved, blow by blow, descriptions of what happened as related usually by a Victim, usually in present tense, and over and over again at varying intervals. In his story about what happened the Victim is innocent, right and wins, and the other party is bad and wrong. Stories are almost always total distortions of what really happened. They are the Victim's attempt to make himself right, and so the Truth of what happened is usually the opposite of the history.

THINK: The third element of the Causal Sequence. The mind and everything that exists and occurs in the mind, including thoughts, ideas, memories, dreams, imagination, creativity, taking, analysis, remembering, memorizing or planning.

Trigger, Trigger Event: Any change or movement of anything that activates a NIR Mass, which consists of a Negative Nuclear IDentity, a creation of BAD to be that way, and a charge of Negative Emotion that is experienced as unpleasant emotion. See Event.

UPS: Unhappiness, Pain, and Suffering: The experience (BE-FEELing) of any of the Negative Nuclear Energies that produce Negative Emotion to Self in the form of the negative, painful emotions.

Value: Third component of the Nuclear Energy of Life. The ability to estimate, esteem-ate, evaluate and assign relative values to things, especially to self, where it is self-esteem. As IDentities, it includes worthiness+/-, deservingness+/-, good <> bad, superior <> inferior, more <> less than, etc.

Victim: A person living in the Fatal IDentity that s/he is not Cause, and so Assigns Cause for his/her (negative) experiences or results to an external agent. A person who denies responsability for anything s/he FEELs, THINKs, DOes, or HAVEs, including anything that "happens to happen" to him/her. A Victim denies responsability both as the original Cause of a situation; and as being able to respond, to stop, avoid or remedy the negative effects. The Victim therefore believes that others are doing things to him/her without his participation (Cause); and furthermore, that s/he has no ability (Cause/ Power) to stop or avoid those things. The Denial of Responsability Creates Victim.

Victim in Relationships: The attempt to manipulate others and obtain energy by pretending helplessness, injustice, or that it is their duty to do so. The Victim uses tactics of programming, blame, guilting, emotional blackmail, "you owe me", etc.

What Is; What Is As It Is: The exact things that exist or occur, exactly as they are with nothing added or subtracted in the description. The Facts, Reality, Truth.

Wisdom: The first component of the Nuclear Life Energy. The ability to distinguish what is truly important and knowing how to get it. Wisdom is the ability to foresee the consequences of action. Wisdom includes consciousness, knowledge, intelligence, intuition, and creativity.

Acknowledgments

From Victoria,

This book is published as I celebrate the fiftieth anniversary of my birth. As I reflect on the first half century of my life I am overwhelmed with Joy and Love for the many souls who have assisted me in my journey thus far, whether you know me as Candy, Pauline or Victoria. Some of you taught me to laugh, some of you taught me to cry. All of you taught me some small or not-so-small lesson of life. I am privileged to call you 'family'.

Love and Thanks to,
My dad, Paul Bradshaw
Jeanne & Milton Davis
Shirley Turner
Norwood Turner, Sr.
Lucy and Richard Price

Helen Bradshaw
William Bradshaw
Richard Zucsak
Rev. Fr. Henry Bowen
Rev. Fr. Norman Jalbert
William Kuchle
Elaine Conlon
Alline Powell
Leon Mitchell Powell
Thomas Michael Powell
John Alexandrov
James R. Keane
Cheri Wood
Monsignor Francis Scollen
Jean-Paul Bradshaw-Willey
Chrétien Bradshaw-Willey
Scott R. Willey
Nina and Sieferd Schultz
Sharilyn Bell
Theresa and Tracy Bayer
Florence Cirafice
Rev. Fr. Larry Sullivan
David Saacke
Cindy Richard
Robert C. Jones
Angel Gonzalez
Thomas Lynch
Beatrice Ware
Kathy Van Horn
Betty Fralin

Shayla Manning
Scott Shikora
Patricia Crane, PhD
Rick Nichols

My brothers — Brad, Wayne, Barry and Rodney

And a very special thank you to my mom, Rosalind Price Bradshaw who not only gave me life but continues to give me LIFE even now.

And to Addam and Deven who have eaten way too much take out food while I finish this project – but when you consider my cooking talents you're not complaining are you?

Upon completing this book, you will have learned how to implement strategies and processes that will be a powerful agent of Positive Energy for your organization. But of far more significance to you, your family, and the global community you will discover that the true power in life comes from understanding how life works and how you (and others) can create life as you would desire. If you want new and different results, you need new and different ideas. You must release the human potential that lies dormant in your organization and that lies dormant within you.

Victoria DePaul, retired after 24 years in Corporate America, has an extensive background in Human Resource Management including supervisory, leadership and corporate trainer positions. In The Science of Leadership, Ms. DePaul details the universal strategies now available to executives, managers or anyone seeking to increase their personal Power. Based in personal experience and application the concepts that she introduces in this book are more than theory—they are the proven steps to organizational transformation. An author, speaker, and entrepreneur she now devotes her time and energy to developing people to their highest potential via seminars and consulting services.

Thomas Michael Powell was for 20 years the CEO of a nationwide and executive leadership, labor force and personal development company in Mexico. An ex-university professor of psychology in Mexico, he led extensive research into human behavior to uncover the true causes of personnel problems and reduced production in organizations. He discovered a great quantity of revolutionary information about the inner workings and motivations of the human being, knowledge that empowers people to major breakthroughs in their control of their lives, their relationships, and their happiness. His books, courses, and seminars have been used by universities and businesses throughout Mexico. In 2006, he left Mexico and returned to his native U.S. where he is now impacting American business.